BEYOND THE MOUNTAINS

SOME SCOTTISH STUDIES IN PRAYER AND THE CHURCH

MARTIN REITH

London SPCK

First published in 1979
SPCK
Holy Trinity Church
Marylebone Road
London NW1 4DU

Filmset in Great Britain by
Richard Clay (The Chaucer Press) Ltd,
Bungay, Suffolk
Printed by
Fletcher and Son Ltd, Norwich

ISBN 0 281 03699 3

BEYOND THE MOUNTAINS

TO
*my fellow-members
in the Company of
the Servants of God*

QUOTATIONS

As the very liberal use of capital letters in the past
is now outdated, and can divert modern readers from
the meaning of a passage, I have taken the liberty of
reducing them to a minimum. Spelling has, on
occasion, also been modernized; but no words have
been changed. Where an explanation of a word is
required, it has been inserted by me in *square*
brackets.

All quotations from the Bible, unless otherwise
stated, are from the Revised Standard Version.

CONTENTS

ACKNOWLEDGEMENTS

I am very especially grateful to the Revd D. Mackinnon, parish minister, Kyle of Lochalsh, for making translations of poems which I had chosen from the Fernaig manuscript. Only two poems and a couple of verses have, to my knowledge, ever been published in English before from this Gaelic anthology.

I am also very grateful indeed to the late Revd Canon W. D. Cooper, BD, for placing at my disposal his unsurpassed knowledge of the Episcopal Church in the eighteenth century.

And I am grateful also to the Revd Father Robert, CSWG, and the Revd Mother Mary Clare, SLG, for reading various chapters on prayer, and for their encouragement. And similarly to my former colleagues on the Oxgangs Christian Council, the Revd J. Orr and the Revd C. Kelly, for their comments on Chapter 9.

Once again I am indebted to the Revd G. R. D. McLean for his most generous permission to quote freely from his *Poems of the Western Highlanders*. And I should like to thank Dr J. L. Campbell of Canna for his permission to reproduce verses from his *Fr Allan McDonald of Eriskay*, and Miss B. Fairweather for allowing me to quote from *A Short History of Ballachulish Slate Quarry*.

Thanks are due to the following for permission to quote from copyright sources:

A. S. Ross & Company: *History of the Clan Macrae* by A. Macrae

Blackie & Son Ltd: *The Literature of the Highlands* by M. Maclean

Dr Eleanor H. Hull: *Poem Book of the Gael* published by Chatto & Windus Ltd

Faber & Faber Ltd: *Richard of St Victor: selected writings on contemplation* by C. Kirchberger

Iona Community: *St Columba of Iona* by Lucy Menzies

Thomas Nelson & Sons, UK Ltd: *Adomnan's Life of Columba* by A. O. and M. O. Anderson

Scottish Academic Press: *Carmina Gadelica, Hymns and Incantations, with Illustrative Notes on Words, Rites, and Customs Dying and Obsolete*

Stirling Tract Enterprise: *The Owl Remembers* by John Mackechnie. Poem translated by Patrick McGlynn

Victor Gollancz Ltd: *An Introduction to Gaelic Poetry* by Derick Thomson

INTRODUCTION

The old order changeth, yielding place to new,
And God fulfils himself in many ways,
Lest one good custom should corrupt the world.[1]

How can anything possibly be corrupted by what is good?
The Christian has a simple answer: good things are only
means to an end. Once anything is highly esteemed, it can
become valued for itself. But all God's gifts are given us in
order that we might use them as stepping stones to God
himself, for the genuine good in each one gives us a glimpse
of the goodness of its Creator. Once we rest in these things—
thereby treating them as ends in themselves—we come to a
halt. Thus we miss the best of God's gifts, which is himself.
So no wonder that St John's first letter ends with the
affectionate warning, 'Little children, keep yourselves from
idols.'

Is that not perhaps why we are now experiencing what
may be the world's greatest 'age of change'? For the Bible
tells us that God shakes the world 'in order that what cannot
be shaken may remain.'[2] We are now being vigorously shaken
surely in order to teach us to put our trust in God himself,
and not in any of his gifts—however helpful or wonderful
the latter may be. If this God is trustworthy then—and only
then—have we security indeed. We are not thereby told the
meaning behind life's problems, but we are offered something
far better—a personal relationship with the invisible God.

Especially in troubled, uncertain times, people want
assurance. Hence the frequent use these days of those words
'relevant' and 'authentic', meaning practical and reliable.
Hence the young hitch-hiker's typical question, as he sat
down beside me in the car and said politely, 'why do you
believe in God?'

To many people, however, Jesus' standard of behaviour is something they can accept at least as a worthy ideal in a very unstable world. For them the problem may well be the Church. As a genuinely perplexed man asked, 'Here—what's the connection between the General Assembly and the Carpenter of Nazareth?' He could have mentioned any church gathering; that one happened to be in the news. The same attitude was described more concisely by another young man, who referred approvingly to a book, for he said it was 'about Christianity as opposed to religion.' (Note the word 'opposed'.)

Unless people believe that they can see the authentic marks of Christ in the Church on earth, they will turn down 'institutional religion' as an empty sham. There may be plenty of hypocrites outside the Church, but those of us who happen to be in it had surely better make certain that we are 'keeping ourselves from idols'.

That Jesus did establish some kind of visible community life is absolutely clear in the Bible. The communal life is to give structure—backbone—not least to help people to fulfil the demands of loving God and each other. But as Norman Macleod put it over a century ago, 'nothing in government, creed or mode of worship can satisfy the increasing hunger in the Church.'[3] For what is meant to be the enabling structure—the invisible skeleton—of the visible Church, will become a restrictive, defensive crab-shell wherever a real, live and vital relationship with God is absent.

If that has happened, no wonder many people cannot see the inner, spiritual life of the Church at all. So the young go off to the Far East in the hope of learning something authentic about God that will be relevant to their lives.

Now Burns wrote,

> O wad some Pow'r the giftie gie us
> To see oursels as others see us![4]

And in a new book about 'the Third World' come two vivid stories about western Christians. In the first some Indians, we are told, decided to study the Bible. They began with St John's Gospel and read its first line, 'In the beginning was the word.' ' "My," said one of the Buddhist monks, "even in the beginning you Christians didn't have a little time for silence!" '[5]

The other story comes from the South Pacific. 'Before the missionaries came, my people used to sit outside their temples for a long time meditating and preparing themselves before entering ... and afterwards would again sit a long time outside, this time—as they put it—to "breathe life" into their prayers. The Christians, when they came, just got up, uttered a few sentences, said Amen and were done. For that reason my people called them Haolis—"without breath"—meaning, those who failed to breathe life into their prayers.'[5]

Can one always blame people for not knowing about the tradition of deep Christian spirituality? Here is but one passage from Thomas Merton: 'In the "prayer of the heart" we seek first of all the deepest ground of our identity in God. We do not reason ... We seek rather to gain a direct existential grasp, a personal experience of the deepest truths of life and faith.'[6]

This silence, this depth, this personal reality, has far-reaching consequences. As a contemporary Orthodox puts it, 'unless and until a man has gained some measure of inward silence, it is improbable that he will succeed in converting anybody to anything.'[7]

Now many coloured threads have gone into the weaving of Scotland's richly diverse heritage. It is like tartan, with sombre but also very bright colours. As good and evil are inextricably interwoven, so are these threads. But there are many elements in our rich Christian heritage that are little or only vaguely known. And in the following studies we shall take a look at some of these. They have much to teach us today.

If a person naturally lives largely by the light of his own experience, then surely a nation must do the same. And we shall find how surprisingly modern were some of our forefathers, facing very similar problems to our own. Each one of them, like us, had to get his own first-hand experience of God. And they too, from the very beginning, had to grapple with the problem of institutionalism in religion.

One of their best-loved Psalms was 121:

I lift up my eyes to the hills.
From whence does my help come?
My help comes from the LORD
   who made heaven and earth.

The hills, the mountains, and all God's gifts point us to their Creator. So we will look at some of them. But we shall look only in order to go beyond them—to God himself—to our fundamental, basic, reliable security and hope in a shaking world.

The pattern of our studies

We shall begin by considering, What were the *first Christians* in this country like? And what was their Church like? They seem to have possessed a unique zest and vitality, and their Church's major crisis developed over the question of institutionalism.

They had a vivid sense of God, so we shall next consider him—as they did too—in his *creation*. At a time when mankind is polluting God's world as never before, we shall use Highland poetry and prayers to help to deepen our own awareness of him in what he has made.

The highest form of God's creation is a saint—a Christlike man or woman. So we shall try to answer, purely from our own original source of information in Scotland, Why has *Columba* made so great an impact on Scots for fourteen centuries?

To follow Christ, where do we start? Presumably from where we are right now—in an upset world—like the men who contributed poetry to the *Fernaig manuscript* during a former 'age of change'. Hardly any of these Gaelic poems have been published before in English. 'We find here, as

4

nowhere else,' writes Dr MacInnes, 'the living heart of Highland piety during a period usually reckoned by evangelicals as spiritually destitute.'[8] For there are plenty of surprises for anyone who is prepared to find spiritual inspiration wherever he can.

In order to have a personal relationship with God we need the 'Mary' element in our lives as well as the 'Martha'. 'Be still, and know that I am God.'[9] Mary was commended by Jesus for sitting still at his feet, looking, loving, listening, contemplating in wonder the Source of all goodness, beauty, and truth. It is doing what George Garden, in his little-known letters from Aberdeen, calls *'the prayer of silence'*. Easy, you think? 'Could you not watch one hour?'[10] said Jesus to his friends. Not even one hour? For significantly their 'watching' was to be a small sharing in his agony in Gethsemane. We naturally shy off that kind of thing, and the devil will provide us with every excuse. The more God asks of us, the more costly becomes the offering.

From this introduction we go on to consider the teaching on *contemplative prayer* by one of Christendom's more famous teachers, Richard of St-Victor. This Scotsman, though writing from abroad, gives us not only instruction for everyone who takes seriously 'the prayer of silence', but also a glimpse of the inner life of some of the great Border abbeys during their early days. For prayer is prayer, whether outside the cloister or in it.

In order to encourage his hearers Richard emphasizes the joy of prayer. So we next examine a *traditional Gaelic poem* which indicates both the hidden joys and also the trials that are necessary if our characters are to be developed. If a sick body needs medical treatment—even operations—to get fit, so does a soul need spiritual training if it is to be enabled to enjoy intimacy with God. And this includes many 'ordinary' experiences.

From the inner, hidden life of Christians we consider once more their communal life in *the Church*. And this time we examine a body of Christians who anticipated not only current trends in Christendom, but those of our own future.

Any study of Church life since the Reformation will inevitably raise the question of Christian *unity*. So next we consider briefly a contemporary experiment in drawing different denominations together, not by ecclesiastical politics, but through silent prayer.

Finally, as we look to the future, we bring these studies to an end with a magnificent hymn. It was written by Norman Macleod, latterly of Glasgow, on the subject of *courage*.

Bundaloch, Wester Ross   MARTIN REITH

1 SPRING FRESHNESS
The first Christians in Scotland and their Church

As the hand is made for holding and the eye for seeing,
    thou hast fashioned me for joy.
Share with me the vision that shall find it everywhere:
    in the wild violet's beauty;
    in the lark's melody;
    in the face of a steadfast man;
    in a child's smile;
    in a mother's love;
    in the purity of Jesus.[1]

That prayer is of the twentieth century. After slight adaptation it can be used in an urban setting as easily as in a crofting township or holiday cottage. Its scope is universal and ageless.

It assumes the existence of a benevolent Creator who is very great indeed because the whole of the vast universe was made by him. Yet he is also very close to us—his life pulsating through all life—and his beauty expressing itself in all beauty, but above all in the sheer perfection of Jesus.

Even in its ageless, timeless quality, that prayer is characteristically Celtic. And it embodies what increasing numbers of people believe to be the vital, missing ingredient in our modern society—with the latter's rank materialism, its slavery to change, and the inevitable threat of self-annihilation.

The original Celts

First, however, we must consider the original Celts. The name is applied to people who moved westwards across Europe in a series of prehistoric migrations from somewhere in central Asia. Their chief common denominator was their

7

language, despite variations which we today know as Gaelic, Welsh, and other variants. But there was more to it than that, as we should expect from a tribal and pastoral society, which had relatively few material possessions, and lived very close to nature.

These people, judging from pre-Christian Irish verse, were highly sensitive. This is superbly illustrated by the account of the vision of one of their heroes, after he had eaten the legendary Salmon of Knowledge. ' "Finn, what do you see?" And he said that he saw May Day, and the swallows skimming and haze on the lake and the rushes talking, heather and black peat, and the sea asleep.'[2] A people who can perceive how extra-ordinary are the 'ordinary' things in life are in little danger of becoming superficial and sophisticated. It is a matter of seeing into the truth of things. Perhaps it enabled them later the more easily to recognize him who said, 'I am the truth.'

In common with other primitive races they believed that God—to some extent—was a fearsome creature and not particularly moral. He seems to have been thought of as a paramount chief whose activities were however unrestrained by any tribal council, but who did have some sense of responsibility towards his people, mankind. To what extent the Celts revered a super-God, or concentrated their attention on lesser, tribal deities, is uncertain. In any event unseen powers had to be propitiated—whether by gifts to the spirit of a well, or by human sacrifices to more powerful deities. The latter practice seems to have become rare, but it highlights the worshippers' acute knowledge of their dependence on the life force to ensure fertility, and on their need of protection in a world inhabited by other human beings.

Public worship was practised in the open air, which is hardly surprising among migrating peoples who were sensitive to nature. Places of worship, such as forest clearings, would gain a reputation for being sacred simply by association. The people's artistic talent expressed itself especially markedly in bright-coloured enamelled metal-work, and an extraordinary ability was shown for abstract art. The Romans noticed their peculiar use of multi-coloured garments. The folk tales bear the marks of an ancient eastern origin, and altogether we gain a picture of a highly imaginative and vitally alive people. And the tradition of vocal music, which is such a marked characteristic of Celtic peoples today, may well be as old as the race itself.

The concept of the tribe, these days, is usually regarded as something barbaric. It is in fact simply an enlarged family, with an emphasis on human relationships rather than on status, on co-operation rather than on competition. The chief was expected to be a 'father' of his people. In pre-feudal times he was elected, and was not necessarily the same as the war-leader. Religion and education were the special responsibility of the druids, and their observations of nature—especially astronomy—were extraordinarily advanced.

The folk tales of the Celts are frequently centred on a hero-figure. Some of the latter's exploits reveal their barbaric antiquity. But their continued popularity in the Highlands, for example, was no doubt not least due to their insistence on the virtues of courage, fortitude, initiative, generosity, hospitality, and on the need for the strong to protect the weak. They are the tales of a warrior aristocracy in a simple cattle-rearing society, where everyone depended on everyone else for survival. Into such a Celtic society came the first heralds of Christ.

Acceptance of Christ

That a warrior society should have raised objections to worshipping the Prince of Peace would have been natural. Some grumbles have indeed been preserved in extant bardic poetry. But objections came from the chief druids whose power was successfully challenged, as at Inverness by Columba. The really remarkable fact is the way in which Celtic society accepted Christ as its King of kings. If the early Christians in these islands had their martyrs it was

9

thanks to Norse and Anglo-Saxon invaders, not to Celts.

Now the first thing that we notice about the Christian mission to what are now called the Celtic countries, is that the leading figures were Celts themselves. And their methods were characteristic. They brought with them no superior attitude to the culture of the people with whom they wished to share their own joy in Christ. And in this respect it is significant that Patrick did not throw down the pre-Celtic standing stones, but simply carved crosses on them. From this simple act we can trace the development of the magnificent Celtic 'high crosses', with their riot of vitally alive little figures and spiral designs, and their frequent 'circle of glory' symbolizing eternal life in Christ. And whatever was healthy in pre-Christian culture was fostered by the monks.

The story of Patrick teaching the Irish about the Trinity by picking a shamrock leaf is symbolic of his ability to utilize the Celt's deep love of nature when teaching him about his Creator. And in his own writings he appears as a very human person, deeply attached to his Lord, with a very uncomplicated religion.

Origins of Celtic Christianity

In order to understand the phenomenal success of the Celtic mission we need first to look a bit further back. In the earliest days of the Christian Church for anyone to become a member it meant for him or her the courting of martyrdom. When Christianity became the official religion of the Roman empire the Church was inundated by half-hearted 'converts', and standards of devotion to Christ fell. As a result a large number of Christians, sickened by the Church's increasing worldliness, went to live in the Egyptian and other deserts. This was no piece of escapism. They did not forsake a life which had become disagreeable to them, but rather denied themselves the consolations which were diverting them from spiritual combat with evil. To go 'into the desert' is to face yourself, your sinfulness, your nothingness, and the stark reality of spiritual evil. It is also a way of finding your true self, and learning in a vivid way the reality of God and the communion of saints. The restricting concepts of space and time disappear. At the heart of the universe the monk, increasingly purified of self and filled with love, bears before God the world and its needs. Some understanding of this spiritual warfare is essential to the study of Celtic Christianity.

Now the collected sayings of these Desert Fathers, as they were known, were written down, and their fame spread. The pungent simplicity of people who had taken Gospel teaching absolutely literally and found it—to almost everyone else's astonishment—to 'work', could hardly fail to impress.

One young man who felt a similar call to that of the Desert Fathers, but in Gaul or modern France, was Martin (c. 397). After years of fulfilling his desire to be chiefly alone with Christ—and what better company?—he was quite literally stampeded by an enthusiastic crowd into becoming a bishop. And in his subsequent career as the apostle of rural Gaul, he also earned the title of Father of the Celtic Church.

Now Gaul was a Celtic country but Romanized, and therefore a place of towns and roads. Christian churches existed in the towns, and after the collapse of the Roman empire the organized Church was the only defence against civil and administrative chaos. Its officials were in contact with one another, and were among the very few who were literate. As a result the bishops and other clerics provided a kind of civil service, and the Roman genius for administration found a new outlet. Like the civil service the Church began to see itself as a kind of hierarchy, and the bishops—residing in towns—wore imperial purple.

But Martin did not. At church services he wore vestments, but otherwise he went about in one of the old peasants' tunics that monks wore. And he lived in a hut—a hermitage —when he was not taken up with frequent missionary journeys among the unevangelized rural tribes. He was the originator of the monk-missionary, and he would travel with parties of these. Most of his companions would be lay-

11

brothers skilled in agricultural and other crafts; and once a tribal chief had consented to give a piece of ground, a new monastery would be founded and the peaceful, purposeful, communal life of the monks would teach its own message in a fractious world. If Christianity reached Britain via imperial Rome, it was the things of Christ—not of Caesar—that were to remain. The western Celts Christianized their own culture instead of exchanging it for a debased Roman one. And when the Roman empire collapsed it was the Celts of the far west who kept the light of Christ brightly burning, during Ireland's 'Golden Age', and poured missionaries into Europe. As Professor Bieler has written of Columba and Columbanus, 'The work of these two monks and their successors shaped decisively the religious and cultural life of England and of Western and Central Europe for several centuries.'[3]

Monastic community witness

The Christian life, by its very nature, is communal. And the Celtic lands were won to Christ by communities. The pattern made an immediate appeal, especially in the non-Romanized purely rural countries. Here the tribal fort with its rowdy young warriors was matched by a monastic 'fort' with its peaceful, well ordered company of 'warriors of the Lord'. Both settlements were composed of groups of huts, surrounded by a stockade, with a larger central wooden building. In all these 'halls' there was music and feasting: in the former they ate, got drunk, and sometimes brawled; in the latter they fed on Christ and sang psalms.

The monks' religion was joyful. On Sundays they wore white, and assembled for the Eucharist or Holy Communion. The celebrant is said to have worn a chasuble or outer garment of eight colours—one more than was allowed for the king when the number of colours indicated your rank. As in the Eastern Orthodox Church the services were long. One gets the impression that these fully choral occasions, with many psalms and collects and litanies alternating, were simply an expression of sheer joy. Some of their prayers have come down to us, with such phrases as:

> Christ is victor; Christ is king; Christ is Lord of all.[4]

> Refreshed with the body and blood of Christ, we give thanks unto thee, O Lord, at all times ... both now and ever, world without end, Amen![5]

As in eastern monasticism each monk followed his own particular type of vocation. Some prayed and worked on the monastic farmlands, showing the dignity of honest labour, like the Carpenter of Nazareth. Others lived physically, but not spiritually, solitary lives of prayer and penance, like Jesus in his whole nights of prayer and his 'forty days in the wilderness'. They literally lived the truth that Christ is all in all, and witnessed most vividly to the supernatural element in Christian living. Meanwhile others were coming and going, to and from their missionary journeys. Kentigern (or Mungo) would spend the whole season of Lent in solitary prayer, and then emerge to mount a massive mission on foot, leaving two or more monks to settle here and there at some pagan sacred site, and so forming a miniature replica of the mother monastery.

A pattern emerges of a tribal monastery with daughter cells scattered over the tribal lands. An abbot (the word comes from 'abba', father) presided over the whole community. One or more bishops existed, normally in each monastery, as the chief ministers of the sacraments, but the abbot would often be a bishop himself. Like them he would inevitably be a simple monk, wed to poverty, and dressing and going about doing the chores like anyone else. Simplicity of living was venerated, and is superbly expressed by the ancient poem, *King Guaire and the Hermit*, in which the treasures of the court are unfavourably compared with the treasures of nature.

If building styles were simple, copies of the Gospels were decorated with all the Celts' love of colour. The Book of Kells—which was probably at least begun at Iona—has been

13

described as the most beautiful book in the world. Art was at the service of God, and nothing but the best was good enough for the best of all books—the Gospels. Of church decoration we know very little; but Bride's church at Kildare was famous for its paintings and bright embroidered hangings.

Wholehearted response

The way in which thousands of vigorously healthy young warriors embraced the monk's life of poverty, chastity, and obedience is nothing short of remarkable—except when viewed in the light of God's power. They stood no nonsense from their bodies. Cuthbert would wade out into the sea and there sing the psalms all night. He was not an eccentric, but revered in his own day as 'the wonder-worker of Britain'. Columba had a stone for a pillow and his face, we are told, 'ever showed gladness, and he was happy in his inmost heart with the joy of the Holy Spirit.'[6] The Celt has never excelled in the art of compromise. To him life is black and white; and if he chooses to follow the Christian ideal in all its uncomplicated simplicity, half-measures will make no appeal.

We are especially fortunate in that Columba's biography is one of the greatest ever written in the early centuries of Christianity. In studying it one needs to compare both its subject and his times with modern saints and missionary activities. Some years ago two Indians were discussing whether Christ should be portrayed for Indian children as an Indian himself. The older said, 'My generation can remember the first European missionaries in our part of India. We saw Christ in them; and so for us Christ will always appear as a white man.' Our Celtic forefathers very obviously saw our Lord in those great missionaries whose names have come down to us—sometimes with little other information. About Moluag and Maelrubha, for example, we know hardly anything; yet there are church dedications to both of them scattered over most of Scotland.

If Columba's biography seems too full of miraculous events to be credible, readers should examine the well authenticated lives of twentieth-century Christians such as Sundar Singh of India, Apollo of Uganda, John of Kronstad, Padre Pio and a host of others. From personal acquaintance some of us would like to add the late Gilbert Shuldham Shaw who had an especial affinity with the Celtic ethos in Christian spirituality.

Columba embodies so much that is admired by Scots that he could be described as a kind of prototype Scotsman. Like so many pioneer missionaries he came from elsewhere—in his case Ireland. As Gaelic culture, shared by Ireland and Scotland, superseded that of the Picts, it is hardly surprising that an Irish Gael should have made his mark. It has been said that the Scot can combine 'strength with deep tenderness or violence with sentimentality.'[7] Of sentimentality there is not a vestige in Columba; but in his early years he seems to have had violence in superabundance. Yet all that force was canalized into self-discipline and love, and this immensely fearless missionary and seaman is still remembered in Scotland's Gaeldom as 'Columba the kind'. He was deeply involved in politics yet would turn aside—while on his way perhaps to anoint a new king—in order to heal a cottar's sick cow. Everyone mattered. If his toughness evoked people's admiration, his tenderness won their love.

Pilgrimage and mission

The conception of life as a pilgrimage made a great appeal both to western Celtic Christians and, more recently, to the Russian Orthodox. Whether or not this was related, in the former's case, to their forefathers' migrations across Europe, the *Quest for the Holy Grail* and the *Voyage of St Brendan* became popular folk tales among them. The latter legend was current especially among the Gaelic Celts, and others, and it exists in an early form. It is probably based on fact, and in it Brendan sets out with companions into the vast Atlantic. Dependent for guidance on God alone, his party have many adventures. And all over Scotland's Gaeldom—as in Ireland

15

—are remains of hermits' cells. For the physical pilgrimage was but a relatively unimportant aspect of the essential inner pilgrimage in the realms of the spirit. It was western Christendom's equivalent of the Desert Fathers' movement; and perhaps it is only those who can feel the Celt's intense love for his kin and his native countryside, and who know something of the desire to love Christ above all things, who can appreciate at least a little of the spirit that motivated these pilgrims in body and spirit. An intense love of country and kindred can interfere with one's readiness to serve Christ wherever he may choose, and in poetry one gets vivid glimpses of the cost of 'pilgrimage' to men like Columba, who could write longingly for the oakwoods of Derry.

Genuine love for Christ implies a natural desire to share that love with others. Hence this pilgrim spirit, among the Celts, also expressed itself in active mission work. The debt that Europe owes to Celtic Christians is great. And Francis of Assisi may have caught something of his love for creation from his visit to an originally Celtic monastic foundation at Bobbio in Italy.

It is noteworthy too that most of the great English missionaries to Holland and Germany were trained by Celts. This was natural because it was the Scoto-Irish—or Gaelic— mission which was chiefly responsible for the conversion of the pagan Anglo-Saxons. As an English bishop put it, 'Not Augustine, but Aidan, is the true apostle of England.'[8] And Aidan was a monk of Iona.

The Welsh-speaking Christians of Britain had been driven westwards by the invading Angles and Saxons, and those who had not been slaughtered were in little mood to try to evangelize their formidable enemies. Meanwhile, despite Canterbury's claims, the Roman mission in Kent had made relatively little headway. So it was left to Aidan's mission in and from Northumbria to cope with the conversion of most of England, and one intrepid Irishman actually reached the south coast and founded a monastery near Chichester.

The links between Christians in Scotland and Ireland were

very close indeed, and two verses from a well-known ancient Irish hymn vividly capture the atmosphere of the Celtic Church of those days:

Be thou my vision, O Lord of my heart;
naught be all else to me, save that thou art,—
thou my best thought, by day or by night,
waking or sleeping, thy presence my light.

Riches I heed not, nor man's empty praise,
thou mine inheritance, now and always;
thou and thou only, first in my heart,
High King of heaven, my treasure thou art.[9]

Spirit and institution

Like all successful missionaries those of the purely Celtic parts of Christendom saw no reason to change their customs. Virile evangelists, organized (if that term can be used to describe Celts) in tribal monastic communities, could hardly be persuaded to conform to the more institutionalized diocesan church structures that had gradually spread over the Continent and into south-east England. Nor did the Celts relish the prospect of being ruled by Rome via an Anglo-Saxon Canterbury. Celtic monasticism was also bound up with tribal economics, so no one can dismiss the Celts as simply being intransigent.

It was the purely practical question of the date of Easter—now calculated on a different basis by non-Celtic western Christendom—that brought matters to a head. (Varieties of monks' hair-styles, so monotonously mentioned by historians, simply indicated which side you were on.) The differences, in fact, between Martin and the administrative type of bishop in Gaul three centuries earlier, had not yet been resolved. Virile monk-missionaries, and diocesan as distinct from monastic bishops, did not necessarily agree. Spirit-guided evangelists do not always fit into the neat and tidy categories of administrators, while the latter fear for the unity of the Church.

17

While people revered the Celtic bishops, kings increasingly felt the need to conform to the Rome-orientated continental pattern. And the decision at the synod of Whitby in 663 that the kingdom of Northumbria should conform to Rome marked a turning point in the history of Christianity in Britain. This synod was held at the combined monastery and convent over which a woman presided, for the Celts had a high regard for their women-folk and did not suffer from an exclusively masculine form of religion. Hilda of Whitby was one of the great abbesses of the Celtic Church, and in sorrow she bowed to the king's decision. Perhaps she knew that a church does not continue indefinitely with its first fervour, and signs of a possible waning of the old spirit showed that a better organized institution was needed. As Professor McNeill has pointed out, 'Without question, inherent vitality is what is essential to a church: organization is secondary and too easily becomes a hindrance to initiative. Yet the lack of concern for widespread organization may have tended to limit the impact, great as it was, of Celtic monastic culture in Europe.'[10]

Within a century the devastating Norse raids had begun, sacking and pillaging every monastery around the northern coasts of Britain. Attacked from within and without, Celtic Christianity as a distinct institution died out. But its spirit very largely remained.

Life seen as a whole

The Celtic church—as it is usually described—may have been lacking in institutional durability. But its strength lay in its 'peculiar zest and abandon' and in its power to convert. And that power was gained not least by the fact that the Celts set out to convert people's entire lives, and not just a part of them. God was to be found everywhere, and everything was to be offered to him. The result was a healthy outlook, expressed by prayers and other devotional songs in which God and every aspect of life were seen to be woven together in a natural integrated whole. If God sustains his

18

creation, and if nature is a unity, then serious imbalance is going to result if artificial distinctions between body, mind, and spirit are introduced. Such categorizing may be necessary when studying man's nature; if it is allowed to divert attention from the basic unity then further artificial distinctions will be invented—those called 'sacred' and 'secular'. That pitfall the early Christians avoided. And despite a vigorous onslaught on various aspects of Gaelic culture during the last three centuries, we in Scotland are fortunate in having had preserved for us—a hundred or so years ago— a very large collection of traditional prayers.

From these prayers we can see that the hearthstone in each house had become a kind of family altar. When monastic, or later parish church, altars, and those in hermitage chapels, had disappeared in any district—for one reason or another— the place of prayer in the home remained. And owing to that homely tradition we can sense something of the Celtic church's spirit.

In these prayers, which were sung or chanted, there is an interweaving of almost all human activities with the awareness of a very great yet very intimate and loving God. A few short examples will illustrate this.

When rising:

> O God, who from last night's sweet rest dost me convey
> unto the light of joy which is today,
> from the new light of day be thou bringing me
> unto the guiding light of eternity.[11]

When dressing:

> Grant to our souls, we pray thee, thy merciful aiding,
> covering them with the shadow of thy wing even as we
> clothe our bodies.[12]

When kindling the fire (or, these days, turning on the electric radiator):

> God, a love-flame kindle in my heart to neighbours all . . .[13]

19

When going to work:

> 'Tis God's will I would do,
> my own will I would rein;
> would give to God his due,
> from my own due refrain;
> God's path I would pursue,
> my own path would disdain.[14]

And so on through the day, till the evening, when such prayers as these might be used:

> O God, for ever praise be to thee
> for the blessings thou bestow'st on me—
> for my food, my work, my health, my speech,
> for all the good gifts bestowed on each,
> O God, for ever praise be to thee.[15]

> The dwelling, O God, by thee be blest,
> and each one who here this night doth rest;
> my dear ones, O God, bless thou and keep
> in every place where they are asleep.[16]

> I am going now into the sleep,
>   be it that I in health shall wake;
> if death be to me in deathly sleep,
>   be it that in thine own arm's keep,
> O God of grace, to new life I wake ...[17]

These prayers reveal a deeply intuitive sense of the Trinity. This one covers all our needs:

> God with me protecting,
> the Lord with me directing,
> the Spirit with me strengthening,
>   for ever and for evermore ...[18]

Homeliness, and an awareness of the unseen dimension of life, appear again and again:

Who are the ones at my helm-tiller near?
    Peter and Paul and John Baptist are they;
at my helm the Christ is sitting to steer,
    the wind from the south making our way.[19]

Sunday was a day of joy. And, as at the wedding of Cana, so

The King of kings
with us in might,
Christ Jesus dear ...[20]

would be present at a party. And a common phrase in poems in praise of a bride—'the beauty of God is in thy face'[21]—at once overcomes modern man's dilemma, as he swings to and fro between puritanism and permissiveness.

As in all folk traditions these prayers, taken together, reveal a mixture of very ancient as well as newer material. Some—perhaps even very much—of the purely Christian prayers may well date from the earliest times. That fairies, for example, should be mentioned on occasion is perfectly natural; to our forefathers they were part of life, and if part of life then part of prayer.

It was the abuse of some of these prayers, by the turning of them into charms, that evoked most hostility to this tradition. For charms are akin to magic, and are used therefore to try to get God—or some other unseen power— to fit in with man's wishes. In Christian prayer, however, man seeks guidance and strength to fit his own life in with God's. And, as so often in history, the throwing out of the dirty bath water, by zealous reformers in any profession, has too often tended to include the baby. Here, only in a few islands are any of the traditional prayers still used. Copies of Dr Carmichael's large nineteenth-century collection of Scottish Gaelic prayers, and smaller anthologies of his or other English translations from his *Carmina Gadelica*, are scattered around the world and prayers from them are certainly used by individuals to the enrichment of their lives.

Writing of the Celtic church Professor Macquarrie states that:

At the very centre of this type of spirituality was an intense sense of presence. The Celt was very much a God-intoxicated man whose life was embraced on all sides by the divine Being. But the presence was always mediated through some finite this-worldly reality, so that it would be difficult to imagine a spirituality more down-to-earth than this one.[22]

The horrifying pitfalls of speculative theology were thus avoided.

The disappearance of the Celtic church was no doubt inevitable. But 'its greatest and lasting value is expressed over and over again in its poetry, which places purity of spirit and integrity of heart above all formal regulations.' So wrote Dr Chadwick, and added that the Celts 'had no towns, no currency, and no large-scale industries or fleet ... Their wealth lies in their spiritual and intellectual endowments.'[23]

Celtic tradition and the modern world

In a world of increasing specialization, in which people are learning 'more and more about less and less', there is an ever greater need for a sense of wholeness. With improved communications the world has become a global village, yet people still lack that sense of the unity of creation that is such a prominent feature in Celtic spirituality.

The awareness of this unity prevents our exploitation of natural resources, for man is part of creation and therefore must co-operate with—and not try to force—nature. To keep the balance of nature means to adapt one's pace to a natural rhythm; this results in a harmony in which some forms of increasingly common neurosis, for example, cannot exist.

At a time when the extraordinary motto 'bigger and better' is leading to a dehumanization of life, the Celtic tradition stands for 'small is beautiful'. Its traditional villages, cottages, and chapels stand in marked contrast to cities, factories, and large churches. And while no one would suggest that Britain should try to adopt a crofting economy, we do need the Celtic sense of values. For the Celt has developed a civilization on the minimum of wealth, thus emphasizing the truth of Christ's teaching about riches. With his human values he has been able to develop community life, whether in the home, the village, the monastery, or the tribe. It was clan, not class, that once provided the unity. Co-operation, not competition, was the rule. Each person matters. That Christ died for each one of us was, and is, a very acceptable concept. The individual therefore counts. When factory workers are persuaded of this they are less likely to strike. When local government really is local, people develop a sense of responsibility.

The Celt may never have excelled at developing institutions, but in an age when structures in government, industry, and even the Church are increasingly criticized for crushing the spirit that ought to exist in them, the Celt has something very vital to contribute. The current development of the 'house church' and Christian cell movements are entirely in keeping with Celtic tradition.

In ancient times the Celt incorporated many elements into his own way of life, and has kept them. In Gaelic culture traditions which are thousands of years old rub shoulders quite naturally with recent developments. This gives the community roots, and a stability in a changing world. When time is correctly evaluated, it no longer dominates; and the conception of eternity is more easily grasped. Under such circumstances people can afford, unselfconsciously, to be their natural, unsophisticated selves.

'For what shall it profit a man, if he shall gain the whole world, and lose his own soul?'[24] said Jesus. The Celt has never been much use at gaining, dominating, exploiting the world. But he has had remarkable success in adhering to those deeper spiritual and human values which are essential for the development of the very soul of the individual and of the nation.

23

To what extent is all that still true today? One can indeed see it vividly in the lives of individuals, and even in families and larger communities. But is that spirit, based on those values, still as strong as it was in the early days of Celtic Christianity? Above all, is it strong enough—positive enough —to withstand contrary influences in a rapidly shrinking world, in which smaller communities are fast disappearing? It is only when we value the best in our heritage that it can be not only handed down from generation to generation, but shared with others in a desperately needy world.

2 *GOD IN CREATION*
Some reflections in the Highlands

Hark! the sea comes shore-ward rolling,
Like a dear friend's step, but softer,
With its wavelets rising, falling,
Like the chubby cheeks of laughter.

Oft did I aforetime ponder
What might be their secret meaning,
Ferried from the ocean yonder
Towards the hard shore, shrilly keening.

As their music softly sounding
Reached my ear, each moment sweeter,
Then I felt that awe abounding
Which no human tongue can utter.[1]

So wrote Donald Mackechnie, adding that he knew not the
cause of his awe. But Alistair Maclean did:

I sit upon the shore, Father, watching the face of the
waters and the sun-bright clouds; and the mystery of being
stills my heart to awe. Then I think of Thee, and then,
though mystery lingers, my fear of it is gone. I say to
myself that, beyond the empires of space and light, reaches
Thy power to be my friend. Wherever I go, whether
through a strange land or upon the dark sea-breast, Thou
art with me. Therefore I may be quiet of mind.[2]

Everyone who appreciates art, in any of its forms, will be
aware that the artist is always even greater than his work. A
really great painting, sculpture, piece of music, or poem
simply gives us a glimpse of what is in the mind of the
genius who produced it. The Hebrews knew that well over
two thousand years ago, and sang 'the heavens are telling the

glory of God; and the firmament proclaims his handiwork.'[3] And when God appeared to us in human form, in the person of Jesus, he told us to 'look at the birds'. Why? In order to catch a glimpse of their and our Creator. 'They neither sow nor reap ... and yet your heavenly Father feeds them,' he taught. And again, of the wild flowers, 'consider the lilies ... even Solomon in all his glory'—in all the worldly splendour of his wealthy court—'was not arrayed like one of these.'[4] And St Paul was later to write that 'ever since the creation of the world his [God's] invisible nature ... has been clearly perceived in the things that have been made.'[5]

Now all this Bible teaching may seem obvious. But down the ages the glories of God's creation have been appreciated only too often without a thought being given to their Creator. In fact the current threat of human annihilation, through exploitation and pollution of natural resources, is a vivid reminder that too many people have slipped into a state that is worse than pagan. For at least primitive man respected nature, and even worshipped some of the more beautiful objects in God's creation.

In sun-worship we catch a glimpse of a primitive realization that life is sacramental. In other words that the presence of something invisible is indicated by some physical object which we can see. This traditional, and probably very ancient, Gaelic poem makes this clear:

Thou sun of joy, glory to thee,
To thee be glory, O thou sun,
Face of the God of life to see,
Face of the morning rising one,
    To thee be glory, O thou sun.[6]

These days we can see so much more of God's creation than our ancestors were able to do. We have telescopes, microscopes, and radar. And yet who is blind? They who looked through what they saw to its Source, or we who can see no more than our physical—and mechanically aided—eyes can perceive? Our earliest Christian Gaelic forebears not only felt the Creator's life-force pulsating through the whole of nature, but knew their God through Christ.

> The gleam of distance, the gleam of sand,
>   Roar of waves with a tide that sings
> To tell us that Christ is born at hand,
>   Saving Son of the King of kings,
>   Sun on the mountains high ashine
>   Reveals him divine,
>   Ho! ro! joy let there be![7]

And despite a puritanical fear of enjoying life, which has in more recent centuries at times marred Christian witness, there have always been those who could appreciate the sacramental beauty of nature. Alexander Munro's seventeenth-century songs were very popular in the Highlands, and in one of them he wrote,

> The wonder of the working of creation
> performed by him at the beginning of time;
> epistles each can read,
> the power of God written in the world.[8]

The hills are the most noticeable feature of the Highlands, and the late Lachlan MacBean wrote these verses in his hymn, *The Mountains*:

> Lord, who madest the mountains,
>   Thou art here though unseen;
> Give me also this calmness,
>   Make my spirit serene.

> Strong and steadfast, the mountains
>   Feel no changes of time,
> God did lay their foundations,
>   He hath made them sublime.

> He hath clothed them with beauty,
>   Sweet and lovely and rare,

> By the touch of his fingers
>   They are heavenly fair.
>
> Peace and power and beauty
>   Vale and mountain disclose,
> Dimly showing his glory
>   From whose hand they arose.[9]

While looking up at mountains one can sense God's majesty. His intimacy is also vividly reflected by nature when one looks down and sees

> The speckled bee that flies, softly humming,
>   From flower to flower of the lonely strath.[10]

In the hills, to climb eagerly to the 'high tops'—as in other experiences of life—has its dangers. The goal can not only divert attention from the pleasures of the way, but the view from the top—of other mountain peaks—further diverts attention from the one you are actually on. For a mountain, like God, can not only give a sense of fatherly strength, but also of motherly care. It is providing a home for a multitude of creatures, most of whom do not reveal their presence to arrogant man who thinks he owns God's earth—and especially so if man is in a hurry.

It is not surprising therefore that Duncan Ban MacIntyre's most famous eighteenth-century nature poetry concentrates on one mountain alone, his beloved Ben Dorain.

> My Misty Corrie, by deer frequented,
> My lovely valley, my verdant deli,
> Soft, rich and grassy, and sweetly scented
> With every flow'r that I love so well . . .[11]

In traditional style, by a choice use of Gaelic words, he simply paints an accurate word-picture of the beauties he sees. Occasionally, even in English translation, there is a choice phrase such as

> And the white dawn melted in the sun, and the red deer cried around.[12]

Suddenly to come, unexpectedly, upon deer in the hills is like being allowed to share in God's enjoyment of his own creation. And MacIntyre's love for these creatures of the wild is especially noticeable in his poem *Ben Dorain*.

> How many thy slim hinds,
>   Their wee calves attending,
> And, with white-twinkling tails,
>   Up the Balloch ascending ...[13]

The whole long poem needs to be read to savour this poet's acute perception of the habits and appearance of the deer, and his intense love for them.

As a professional hunter MacIntyre inevitably spent much time alone, silent and motionless. In such conditions sensitivity can develop. Distracting noise will lessen the perception of intense beauty, such as at the sudden sight of a galaxy of white water-lilies on a peat-black lochan. And stillness is required if many of nature's objects are to be noticed at all. Scents, like those of the bog-myrtle, or birches on a warm June evening, are obvious. But it requires complete silence and attention to hear many of the sounds of nature and recognize them. At night, when the eye cannot function, a whole new world of sound will present itself. Awareness, as in prayer, grows with stillness, alertness, and experience.

For most of the year most people of course can only see the Highlands in photos. One can forget how many hours of perseverance and acute discomfort may have gone into the production of a really good nature photograph. As in prayer, what God provides has to be worked for. The gift of himself is constant. Sometimes, like a pine forest on a winter's day, sorrowful experiences may make him seem dark and forbidding. Only when one draws close to the trees— sometimes after the effort of tramping through deep snow— one finds that they are always green.

Then there is the tranquil beauty of form in nature. In a built-up area wherever you look your eyes are jolted against straight, vertical lines. In the country, or among natural things in a garden, there is the gentle flowing of outlines. Even when the eye meets a tree-trunk it is at once led away along a branch, round leaves, to a curved skyline, the sea's horizon or soft-edged clouds. The outward peace can be extremely intense, and perhaps rarely more so than during a Highland autumn on a still evening. Like golden fountains the weeping birches are perfectly mirrored in the glass-like lochs, and white mist hangs motionless about the hill-tops.

For Evan MacColl the winter made a great appeal, and his poem 'To the falling snow' turns his reader's attention to aspects of beauty most city-dwellers may not have noticed.

> Bright-robed pilgrim from the North!
> Visitant of heavenly birth,
> Welcome on thy journey forth—
>   Come, come, snow!
>
> Light as fairy footsteps free,
> Fall, oh fall! I love to see
> Earth thus beautified by thee.
>   Come, come, snow!
>
> Silent as the flow of thought,
>   Gentle as a sigh love-fraught,
>   Welcome as a boon long sought,
>   Come, come, snow!

And in his descriptions of the beautifying effects of snow is this verse:

> Streamlets that to yonder tide
> Gleam like silver as they glide,
> Look like darkness thee beside:
>   Come, come, snow![14]

Poets write chiefly about the beauties of nature. But there is the desolation too. In a town it is possible to live an escapist life, for there are so many distractions. In the wilds, in stillness and loneliness a person will be brought face to face with himself, with his lack of inner resources, with his nothingness. But he also has the chance of discovering God in creation, and in the depth of his own being. And from that discovery it is easier to find God in others.

However beautiful any facet of nature may be, one cannot escape the fact of its original birth-pangs. The beauty of crystalline rocks has resulted from intense heat, and Highland land-forms have been produced largely by the action of ice. And this extract from a Gaelic poem by Allan McDonald is a vivid description of nature's challenge to man to develop ingenuity and fortitude.

> Rough, gloomy weather, as is usual in early February; white spindrift off the sandbanks driven everywhere; spray like ashes driven across the Sound; sod and slate loosened by the quick blows of the wind. Fierce squalls from the north shaking every gable, hard hailstones which would cut the top off one's ears, men so chilled with cold that they cannot look outside, huddled indoors at the edge of the ashes.[15]

If the beauty of the Creator can be seen in nature, so can his power—and also the truth that man is an exceedingly small object on the face of God's earth. People were very aware of this in olden times, and Alexander MacDonald (Mac Mhaighstir Alasdair) wrote this passage about the crew's journey prayer before setting out in the galley:

> Great Father, that gathered the waters,
> Whose breath is the strength of the storm,
> Bless Thou our frail bark and its men,
> When the rage of the tempest is warm.
> O, Son of the Father, give blessing
> To anchor and rudder and mast,
> To sail and to sheet and to tackle,
> When they stand the rude strain of the blast.[16]

Perhaps it is necessary to acknowledge man's smallness and God's greatness before one can appreciate that nature is —as someone put it—'the hem of his garment'. Then the whole world is seen and felt to pulsate with God's creative energies. And in another poem, Allan McDonald wrote about Eriskay and its significance.

> Beautiful island of whitest strands,
> the whiteness of the wavetops around thy edge,
> winter cannot hurt thee,
> thou art like the Holy Church of God,
> the everlasting rock is thy foundation.
>
> Beautiful island, thou art full of happiness,
> thou art the jewel of the world on a May morning,
> the dew shining like white diamonds,
> glittering brokenly on thy green clothing,
> the picture of the stars on the plain of the heavens.[17]

Those who believe that everything in nature has evolved purely for functional reasons should surely ask themselves if it is really necessary to have so many shades of green in a hazel wood in spring. Or is it necessary, apart from sheer beauty, for wild flowers to come into bloom at a time when their colours compliment each other, like purple bell heather with bluebells (harebells) and yellow bedstraw?

Poets have been impressed time and time again by the sheer beauty of nature alone.

> Passing by the Sugar Brook
> In fragrant morn of May
> When like bright shining rosaries
> The dew on green grass lay.[18]

And that beauty has led the poet to think not only of its Creator, but to do so in the spirit of worship.

If there is beauty, there must surely be a depth of tenderness in a Creator who can produce a young mountain hare. And humour too. Is it not most odd that he who created a sense of humour should so often be denied its possession himself? Just look at a herd of common seals basking on a skerry like so many shiny sausages in a pan, splashing the water with their fore-flippers, or generally swimming around for the sheer fun of it. One fat old bull seal will apparently yawn, as if tired out by his exertions, and wave his tail flippers like someone rubbing his hands together with pleasure over a job well done. But he has been lying there in the sun doing absolutely nothing for several hours. And why not? That's the way seals were made. If he has obeyed the laws, for him, of his Creator, he should have a perfect right to be pleased! It is more than we human beings do.

On the whole the wild creatures reflect God because of their obedience to him. Admittedly it is unconscious; but that does not decrease its object lesson. When the sea is calm, and the islands seem to be floating on it in a tranquillity that must be experienced to be believed, you might notice a school of porpoises go by. Like the top of a wheel, in single file, the huge beasts rise, curve over and dive. With effortless grace and precision timing, the performance is repeated at apparently exact intervals until the school vanishes into the distance. There must be few sights in nature that can give such a vivid sense of the rhythm of an ordered creation. One gets a similar sense with the moon going through its various phases—'the glory-lantern of the poor'[19] as traditional Gaelic poetry calls it.

> Hail to thee, so bright,
> Jewel of the night!
> Beauty of the height,
> Jewel of the night!
> Thou star-mother white,
> Jewel of the night!
> Thou sun-fostered light,
> Jewel of the night!
> Queen-star in thy might,
> Jewel of the night![20]

There is a similar sense of rhythm with the tides, as expressed in another traditional poem.

As it was, as it is, and as it shall be
Evermore, God of grace, God in Trinity!
With the ebb, with the flow, ever it is so,
God of grace, O Trinity, with the ebb and flow.[21]

With his own awareness of God in creation Alistair Maclean wrote:

A bird flies over the sea, and I, wondering, ask whither. Thou answerest, 'I am its guide. I am the strength of its tireless wing. I choose its secret path. I bring it to its rest.' Make me to be still, Lord, with the happy thought that Thou art doing the like for me. Be Thou my refuge and my song ...[22]

If mankind would emulate, with regard to God, the obedience and devotion of a well-trained sheep dog, the world would indeed be blest. We are too often like a stupid ewe whom the Good Shepherd, helpers, and sheep dogs are all trying to guide in one direction—for her own good; but she persists in trying to evade all their benevolent influences.

People whose lives are geared to the rhythm of nature have not a few lessons to teach a disordered world. Only at such a pace can an eighty-year-old crofter scythe a hayfield single-handed.

I will bring praise to the King of grace
For the ground-crops growing in the place,
To us and the flocks food he will give
As he bestoweth that we may live.[23]

The greatest of all God's creatures is of course mankind. And in their early years human beings can reveal some of the most attractive of all character traits. Jesus was very clear on this point. He taught, 'truly, I say to you, unless you turn and become like children, you will never enter the kingdom of heaven.' And again, 'see that you do not despise one of these little ones; for I tell you that in heaven their angels always behold the face of my Father who is in heaven.'[24] That last remark at least implies an especially close relationship between children and God. And sometimes it is those who have no children, like Columba the monk, who see this most clearly and attractively. He is said to have written this verse to a child:

> O conscience clear,
> O soul unsullied,
> Here is a kiss for thee—
> Give thou a kiss to me![25]

On one rainy day some children went out to play. Not content with getting wet from above, they plunged into the burn—which by that time was in spate—and their whole-hearted enjoyment, combined with delighted laughter, was a tonic to watch. The water poured into their wellington boots, and they splashed each other out of sheer hilarity. Had it been a sunny day, they would have enjoyed the sun; but as it was a rainy day, they went out and enjoyed the rain. Adults who can deliberately go out with joy to face whatever God provides or permits have certainly learned how to live.

It is both significant and very homely that when God appeared on earth as a man he began the same way as we do—by being a child. And this traditional Gaelic poem vividly expresses this:

> The Virgin approaching, o behold,
> Doth Christ so young on her breast enfold,
> The angels making obeisance low,
> The King of glory praising it so.[26]

The children's performances are one of the most attractive features of the annual Gaelic Mod or cultural festival. Highland music is extraordinarily evocative of the land of its

35

origin. And not least so in that rarely understood classical music of the bagpipe, the *ceol mor* or 'pibroch'. A master player has been able to bring a hush on thousands of tourists at a Highland Games, as in his playing the mountains and forests seemed to sing.[27] But there is an extraordinary expression too of a mixture of joy and sorrow in this form of music, a mixture which reveals a deep truth about life that reached its mysterious heights in the crucifixion.

But the subject which has probably inspired song writers more than any other is that of falling or being in love. The Gael has some exceptionally beautiful poems on this theme, such as this verse by Norman Macleod (Am Bard Bochd) which incorporates too something of the traditional Celtic nature poetry.

Glen Ramadale;
my love in the dew of twilight;
a morning glory in her hair,
setting it alight;
the hidden cuckoo's call
encircling her.[28]

At least two Christian writers apparently suggested that falling in love is not only a physical-psychological process, but can also be a spiritual experience. For, they maintained, it is God showing someone another person in glory; and if they are meant to marry he is saying 'this is what your partner can become, and I want you to help him/her to reach that glory of character.' Then they marry and the vision fades. The couple may feel that they have simply experienced some form of midsummer madness, and so fail to respond to the God-given opportunity.

Unlike the animals man has no ordered breeding season. In fact in this aspect of his nature he is uniquely disordered. Hence his temptation either to suppress his natural instincts completely, or to give them full licence—which ends in slavery to them; or else to indulge in varying degrees of frequently unsatisfactory compromises. In this respect the traditional Gaelic bridal poems, or verses composed for a bride on her wedding day, show us the sacramental approach to this subject:

> The lovely likeness of God's Son
> Is o'er thy pure face shed upon,
> The likeness loveliest and best
> That ever on the earth did rest.[29]

In all beauty we catch a glimpse of the beauty of God. In remembering this a woman can overcome her vanity, and a man can see her in a new light.

If all creation has its birth-pangs, so does the re-creation of one who accepts his or her call to follow Christ. And Ann Mackellar wrote significantly of her God and Saviour that

> It was in the poor bothy of sorrow
> that I got to know you first ...
> You gave me your love
> in the shade of the juniper tree,
> and the companionship of your affection
> in the garden of the apples.[30]

Nature, conforming to God's natural laws, can be extra-ordinarily beautiful. So can a human character as a person learns to conform to God's moral and spiritual laws. Such people are impossible to describe. They can simply make an impact on others which is as inspiring as it is lasting.

One such person was a widow in South Uist, in the Outer Isles. We met in the open one evening, and soon talked about the things that matter most in life. As we looked out across the Atlantic into a vivid sunset her face glowed, and with radiant smile and intense passion she said quietly, 'God is so good. God is *so good*!' And one felt, had the sunset disappeared, her face would still have shone.

Perhaps she knew this traditional song from her native isle. It seems to express exactly what she, after a long life not devoid of suffering, had become:

37

I sing of the eye so keen and bright,
I sing of the guide-star's shining light,
I sing of the King of all the kings,
I sing of the God of living things,
    Song of King of all the kings,
    Song of God of living things.[31]

3 VISION OF MANHOOD
*Adomnan's 'Life of Columba':
the prototype Scotsman?*

One of the endearing qualities of the Irish is the readiness—
of at least many of them—to criticize themselves. And some
years ago a correspondent in Dublin wrote that they had been
unfortunate in their choice of national heroes. One might
have forgotten that statement if she had not added that the
Scots were in a similar predicament.

There is indeed plenty of scope for a long discussion on that
opinion! We would surely however be agreed that in at the
very least one case the choice—for both countries—has been
most excellent. And that is in Columba. For, as an Irishman
who became one of Scotland's outstanding figures of all times,
our two countries share him, and rejoice in him.

National heroes are hardly unimportant. For generations
of school children are taught to admire them. Their choice
is therefore bound to exercise a profound influence. One
author has gone so far as to say that a Hungarian, St Martin,
was the prototype Frenchman, for his character made such
an appeal that the people of his adoption have been strongly
influenced by it ever since.[1]

Can we in Scotland not say, therefore, that St Columba
was the prototype Scotsman? His appeal continues to make
itself felt, and contemporary Scots of many shades of opinion
can find themselves united in admiration of this man. The
appeal can be so great, in fact, that some describe it as 'his
magic'.

There are at least two easily available biographies of him
which make use of all available evidence.[2] The purpose of our
study here, however, is both to introduce some readers to the
earliest substantial source of information about him and,
from this alone, to try to answer the question, Why has

Columba made such a colossal impact on people now for fourteen centuries?

Adomnan's late seventh-century *Life of Columba*[3] is one of the outstanding books that emerge from Europe's 'Dark Ages'. It is not exactly what we today should call a biography, but rather a collection of stories and anecdotes made by one who succeeded Columba as Abbot of Iona about a century after the founder's death. In one sense however Adomnan is remarkably modern, in that he tries to evaluate his evidence. Over one incident, for example, he writes, 'we have received an account of the facts ... from certain truthful and blameless men of good testimony' who, apparently, claimed to have been eye witnesses of the results of a miracle attributed to Columba. [II 9] (The references in parentheses are to the section in Adomnan's *Life* from which each quotation is taken.)

The story of the saint is well known. He was born in Ireland, of royal blood. Hot-tempered and imperious, when already a monk he sparked off a particularly bloody clan battle.[4] Perhaps as a penance he left his intensely loved native land to throw in his lot with the little Irish colony in what is now Argyll. With a party of devoted followers he founded the internationally famous monastery of Iona. How much he can be held responsible for mission work among the Picts is debatable. It doesn't concern us here. In fact if Columba had never put a foot out of Iona he would still have been Columba. That is what surely really matters about him. And that is exactly what Adomnan is trying to describe.

Why was Columba greatly loved?

The answer to that question is simple: he himself greatly loved others. And this constant caring, on his part, is revealed by a number of characteristic incidents. 'On a very cold winter day the holy man was afflicted with great sorrow' we are told. He said to his attendant, Diormit, ' "Not without good cause, my son, do I grieve at this hour, when I see that Laisran is now harassing my monks in the construction of a large building, although they are exhausted with heavy labour; and it vexes me greatly." ' At that moment Laisran, who was in Ireland, ordered the monks to cease work. Columba's love, both for God and for man, gained him the reputation for being able to achieve such results. [I 29]

A similar story comes from Iona itself. For several days a number of monks shared an experience as they returned, tired out, from harvesting. At a place half way to the monastery, they felt—as one of them put it—' "a kind of inspired joyousness of heart, strange and incomparable, which in a moment miraculously revives me, and so greatly gladdens me that all grief and all labour are forgotten. Moreover, the load that I bear upon my back, however heavy it may be, is so greatly lightened (how, I do not know), from this place until we reach the monastery, that I feel no burden." ' The reason for this was explained to them. Baithene said, ' "You know that our senior, Columba, thinks of us with solicitude and, mindful of our labour, is much distressed when we are late in reaching him. And for the reason that he does not come in the body to meet us, his spirit meets us as we walk, and in this fashion refreshes and gladdens us." ' [I 37]

In true Christian fashion all rules were subordinated to the 'rule of love'. ' "Tomorrow",' said Columba, ' "we propose to fast; but nevertheless a disturbing guest will arrive, and the customary fast will be relaxed." ' [I 26] And he would give people detailed instructions about their family affairs. Thus he ordered a murderer to do seven years' penance, then return to a master who would release him from slavery, and finally to take care of his aged father. [II 39] In fact his compassion gave people confidence. Once, in Ireland, Columba walked surrounded by a great crowd. 'Meanwhile, a boy of the congregation, much looked down upon for his countenance and bearing ... came up behind ... intending to touch ... but the hem of the cloak in which the blessed man was wrapped. But this was not concealed from the saint

41

... So he suddenly stopped; and putting out his hand behind him he took hold of the boy's neck, pulled him forward, and made him stand before his face. When all those that stood by said, "Send him away!" ' Columba replied, ' "My son, open your mouth, and put out your tongue." ' And after blessing it, he said, ' "Although this boy appears to you now contemptible and of very little worth, yet let no man despise him on that account. For from this hour not only will he not displease you, but he will greatly please you. And he will grow by degrees from day to day in good ways, and virtues of the soul ... His tongue also will receive from God eloquence, with healthful doctrine." This was Ernene, Crasen's son, famous afterwards among all the churches of Ireland.'[I 3]

Naturally, the sick were healed. On one occasion his monks brought a young man to him who had been struck suddenly by a serious illness. 'The saint at once took pity upon them, and spread his holy hands to heaven, with earnest prayer, blessed the sick youth', who was thereupon healed.[II 31]

Columba's compassion included all living things. On one occasion a crane landed on Iona. The abbot called one of his monks and said, ' "with its strength almost exhausted it will fall near you and lie upon the shore. You will take heed to lift it tenderly, and carry it to the house near by; and, having taken it in as a guest there for three days and nights, you will wait upon it, and feed it with anxious care." '[I 48] And this love was returned. Just before the abbot's death he was sitting by the wayside, and his white horse 'went to the saint, and strange to tell put its head in his bosom ...'[III 23]

The whole conception of Christian love has been so debased that it is necessary to add that Columba was in no way soft. On one occasion, when a man was apparently shouting for a ferry to fetch him across the sound, the abbot said, ' "Much to be pitied is that man who is shouting and who has come to us to seek things suitable for physical remedies, when today the fitter thing for him was to occupy himself with true repentance for his sins. For in the end of this week he will die." '[(I 27)] But he did not give up his efforts to help the sinful, realizing as he did the inevitable result of living deliberately against God's moral law. So, 'in the dead of night' on another occasion, he said to the monks around him in church, ' "Now let us pray earnestly to the Lord, because in this hour a sin unheard-of in this world has been committed …" '[(I 22)] Nor would Columba take a superior attitude to others' moral lapses. One man came to the saint, and 'kneeling before his feet, he groaned bitterly, with weeping and lamentation, on bended knees, and confessed his sins before all those that were present. Then the saint, as much in tears as he, said to him: "Rise, my son, and be comforted. Your sins that you have committed have been forgiven, because as it is written: 'A contrite and a humbled heart God does not despise'." '[(I 30)]

Columba was always concerned about others. Just before he died he told his monks, ' "I desired with desire to depart to Christ the Lord, as had indeed been granted by him to me, if I had so chosen; but I chose rather to put off a little longer the day of my departure from the world, so that the festival of joy [Easter] should not be turned for you into sorrow." '[(III 23)] And, practical to the end, he rejoiced that at his forthcoming death the monastery would have a year's supply of corn in store.

His insight into human character was penetrating indeed. When a certain priest was consecrating the Elements during the Holy Eucharist, Columba said, ' "Now we see clean and unclean intermingled together: the clean rite of the sacred offering administered by an unclean man, who at the same time keeps hidden in his own conscience a great sin." '[(I 40)] And his concern with people led him into politics. When there were rival claimants to the throne he was on an island, spending days in prayer. As a result of his waiting on God he believed it was his duty to act. So 'he sailed over to the island of Io, and there, as he had been bidden, he ordained as king Aidan, who arrived about that time.'[(III 5)]

Generosity is a virtue especially associated with Columba,

for he did nothing by halves. On one occasion he was offered many gifts and 'he pointed especially to the gift of a rich man, saying: "God's mercy goes with the man whose gift this is, for his mercies to the poor, and his generosity." ' [I 50] And on another occasion, when a thief was brought to him, he said, ' "Why do you repeatedly steal other people's property ... When you have need, come to us, and you will receive the necessary things that you ask for." And saying this, he ordered wethers to be killed, and given instead of seals [from the community's seal colony] to the miserable thief; so that he should not return home empty.' [I 41]

Columba was particular about hospitality. After spending the night with a poor man, he 'questioned his lay host in the early morning about the nature of his property. Thus questioned, he replied: "I have but five little cows; if you bless them, they will become more." He brought them immediately at the command of the saint' who said, ' "God granting it, you shall have a hundred and five cows." ' [II 21] 'But concerning a certain very niggardly rich man' who 'did not receive him as a guest', Columba prophesied, ' "The riches of that greedy man, who has spurned Christ in pilgrim guests, will from this day be gradually diminished, and will be reduced to nothing." ' [II 20]

If generosity was part of Columba's nature, it included generosity over praise. When the saint came across goodness, in any form, he appreciated it. Once in Skye he said, ' "today in this place, on this plot of ground, a certain pagan old man, who has preserved natural goodness throughout his whole life, will be baptized, and will die, and will be buried." ' [I 33] But natural goodness was no substitute for Christ. On another occasion, while travelling along Loch Ness-side, he said, ' "Let us hasten towards the holy angels that have been sent from the highest regions of heaven to conduct the soul of a pagan, and who await our coming thither so that we may give timely baptism, before he dies, to that man, who has preserved natural goodness through his whole life, into extreme old age." ' [III 14] And if we ask what was the nature of the goodness that Columba appreciated so much, we might turn to his comment on a certain iron-smith. Of him he said, ' "See now, his soul is being carried by holy angels to the joys of the heavenly country. For whatever he was able to gain by practising his craft he laid out in alms to the needy." ' (III 9)

His inner life

The chief motivation of all that he did was his love of his Lord. He would refer to his 'much wished-for passing from this world to Christ' (I 2) in order fully to realize his heart's desire for absolute union with God. Meanwhile life had to be lived entirely for God, and he expressed this once by describing two new visitors to Iona. He said, ' "These two strangers, offering themselves as a living sacrifice to God, and consummating in a short space long years of service as soldiers of Christ, presently within this same month will depart in peace to Christ the Lord." ' (I 32)

To live for Christ implies total obedience. And whatever we may make of the following story, it certainly implies that Columba had to learn a costly lesson. We are told that an angel appeared to him and commanded him to consecrate a certain new ruler. 'But when he refused to ordain Aidan as king ... because he loved Iogenan, Aidan's brother, more, the angel suddenly stretched out his hand and struck the holy man with a scourge, the livid scar from which remained on his side all the days of his life.' (III 5) Thus we are not surprised at the kind of orders he gave his monks. For example, with regard to one man he said, ' "in God's prescience it is not predestined for him to become a monk of any abbot ... you will therefore refuse to keep this man with you ... lest you should even seem to oppose the will of God." ' (I 2)

It is hardly surprising therefore that there should be many tales indicating that Columba lived very close to God. Here is perhaps the best known one. 'From the top of the little hill the spy saw him standing on a certain knoll of that plain and

45

praying, with his hands outstretched to the sky, and his eyes raised to heaven, and then ... holy angels, citizens of the heavenly country, flew down with marvellous suddenness, clothed in white raiment, and began to stand about the holy man as he prayed.'[(III 16)] (This place is the Hill of the Angels, on Iona). On another occasion, 'when the rites of the Mass were being celebrated, Saint Brenden mocu-Alti saw ... a kind of fiery ball, radiant and very bright, that continued to glow from the head of Saint Columba as he stood before the altar ...'[(III 17)] And on 'one winter night' when the abbot entered the church a monk saw a 'heavenly brightness' and 'could not at all endure it, because the brilliant and incomparable radiance greatly dazzled his sight.' As was to be expected, in the presence of intense holiness, the viewer was 'greatly overcome by fear'.[(III 19)]

If Columba was at times seen surrounded by light, he certainly lived in the clarity of that light. He once told someone that ' "There are some, although few indeed, on whom divine favour has bestowed the gift of contemplating, clearly and very distinctly, with scope of mind miraculously enlarged, in one and the same moment, as though under one ray of the sun, even the whole circle of the whole earth, with the ocean and sky about it." '[(I 43)] He could see life whole rather than fragmented. And it brings to mind a remark of a modern saint, who wrote, 'in the mind of GOD there is no such thing as division—to Him the whole Mystical Body is one and entire. It is the deranged mind of man that invents division.'[5] And in these days of confusion when even the possibility of certainty about anything is questioned —and despaired of—we notice the reason for Columba's clarity of vision: as Jesus said, 'If any man's will is to do his [God's] will, he shall know whether the teaching is from God ...'[6] And the most vivid example of this in Columba's life is the story of light shining from the house in which he had withdrawn for several days of uninterrupted prayer. It was reported that 'spiritual songs, unheard before, were heard being sung by him. Moreover, as he afterwards admitted in the presence of a very few men, he saw, openly revealed, many of the secret things that have been hidden since the world began. Also everything that in the sacred scriptures is dark and most difficult became plain, and was shown more clearly than the day to the eyes of his purest heart.'[(III 18)]

If Columba saw life whole, he saw something infinitely greater than this earthly life alone. Once he said to someone, ' "Rise, and do not be grieved. You will die in one of my monasteries; and your part in the Kingdom will be with my elect monks, and with them you will awake from the sleep of death into the resurrection of life." '[(II 39)] A loving heavenly Father naturally wants his children for ever; and as Columba said, ' "The omnipotence of God rules all things, and in his name, under his guidance, all our movements are directed." '[(II 34)] All he requires therefore is our trust and obedient co-operation. And this the abbot taught his monks. So, when Columba predicted that 'a great whale' lay in the route Baithene was about to sail, the latter simply replied, ' "I and that beast are in God's power," '[(I 19)] and he set off unafraid.

Columba had no doubt about the cosmic war between good and evil, nor that anyone relying on God's almighty power would be bound to win in his own sector of the conflict. A typical remark of his was ' "Now I have seen holy angels at war in the air against the adversary powers." '[(III 6)] And had not St Paul written, 'be strong in the Lord and in the strength of His might ... For we are not contending against flesh and blood, but ... against the spiritual hosts of wicked-ness ...'?? Hence Columba's conflict in withstanding the powers of evil. He himself spoke of 'demons making war against him', for 'They, as was revealed by the Spirit to the holy man, wished to assail his monastery ... But he, one man against these innumerable enemies, fought a strong fight, taking to himself the armour of the apostle Paul.'[(III 8)] And on another occasion he said, ' "Behold, the woman of whom I spoke in your presence a year ago is now meeting in the air the soul of her husband, a pious layman, and is fighting for it along with holy angels ... aided by the righteousness of the mortal man himself ... [who] has been brought to the place of eternal rest." '(III 10) And by way of predicting a saint's death, Columba ordered his attendant, saying, ' "Let the sacred ministries of the Eucharist be quickly made ready. For today is the blessed Brenden's natal day." '(III 2)

The result of his inner life

We are told that Columba 'was angelic in aspect, refined in speech, holy in work, excellent in ability, great in counsel. Living as an island soldier for thirty-four years, he could not pass even the space of a single hour without applying himself to prayer, or to reading, or to writing or some kind of work. Also by day and by night, without any intermission, he was so occupied with unwearying labours of fasts and vigils that the burden of each several work seemed beyond the strength of man. And with all this he was loving to every one, his holy face ever showed gladness, and he was happy in his inmost heart with the joy of the Holy Spirit.' (Preface)

'One day, while the saint was in the island of Io, he rose quickly from reading, and said with a smile: "Now I must go in haste to the oratory, to plead with [i.e. pray to] God for a certain woman in distress, who now in Ireland cries out ... while racked by the pangs of a very difficult birth ..." Saying this, the saint, moved by pity for that young woman, ran to the church, and bending his knees prayed for her to Christ ...' (II 40) We notice that he spoke 'with a smile', for a joyless Christian is a contradiction in terms.

If love and joy are of the essence of the Christian life, then the love for God will result in a person's trusting him. Hence we find the simple comment that, 'This miracle, the Lord granting it, was performed by virtue of the prayers of the celebrated man; because, as it is written, all things are possible to him who believes.' (II 15) That is faith. And God gives us opportunities to cultivate it. Hence Columba's sudden remark—again 'with a smile'—' "Colman ... is now in great danger in the surging tides of the whirlpool of Brecan ... But the Lord terrifies him thus ... to rouse him to more fervent prayer that with God's favour he may reach us after passing through the danger." '[I 5]

People who trust in their own abilities may get quite a long way in life. Those who have learnt not to trust in themselves but in Almighty God inevitably get a good deal further. And Columba gives one the impression of a man who had become invincible. Faced with any obstacle he simply relied on God. What joy he must have given the Lord! And this attitude is clearly depicted by the story of his famous visit to the king of the Picts, thought to have taken place at Inverness. The purpose of the mission was to obtain permission to preach the gospel in Brude's kingdom. The souls of thousands of people were at stake. And when Brude refused even to let the Christian party in, an obvious crisis had been reached. So, 'when the man of God learned this, he went with his companions up to the doors of the gate, and first imprinting the sign of the Lord's cross upon the doors, he then knocked, and laid his hand upon them. And immediately the bars were forcibly drawn back, and the doors opened of themselves with all speed.'[II 35] Needless to say the pagan king was much impressed, and the requested permission granted.

On another occasion he told his monks, ' "Now let us pray earnestly to the Lord for this people, and for the king Aidan. For in this hour they are going into battle." And after a short time he left the oratory, and looking into the sky he said: "Now the barbarians are turned to flight; and the victory is yielded to Aidan, unhappy though it is." '[I 8] The problem over praying for soldiers in battle is easily solved: one must always pray that God's will, in every situation, be done. Naturally one will want one's own side to win, and there may be excellent reasons why it should—as with the Allies against the Nazis. All has to be placed trustingly in God's hands. And the more that is at stake, the harder that can be.

Hence our recourse to any and every means to solve our

49

difficulties, except prayer. In this respect Columba's success should surely act as a vital lesson. One day he was faced with a marriage problem, in which the wife 'had an aversion' to her husband 'and would not allow him to enter into marital relations.' Nor could Columba persuade her. She was willing to manage the house alone, or enter a convent. 'Then the saint said: "What you suggest cannot rightly be done. Since your husband is still alive, you are bound by the law of the husband ..."' Impasse? It would appear so. But Jesus said, 'All things are possible to him who believes.'[8] And Columba knew it; and believed it. So he said, ' "let us three ... pray to the Lord, fasting." ' They agreed to this, 'And on the night following, in sleep, the saint prayed for them.' On the next day Columba asked the wife if she still wanted to leave her husband, and 'she said: "I know now that your prayer concerning me has been heard by God. For him whom I loathed yesterday I love today. In this past night (how, I do not know), my heart has been changed in me from hate to love." ' (II 41)

It is hardly surprising that people who knew Columba came to value prayer, for by his example he led them in the paths of the Spirit. And on one occasion during 'a mighty storm' at sea, 'the sailors said to him, as he tried with them to bail the water out of the ship: "What you are doing now does not very greatly profit us in our danger. You should rather pray for us who are perishing." ' (II 12) And that was his chief work, not least 'when he was awake on winter nights, and when he prayed in remote places, while others rested ...' (III 16)

For anyone to be filled with such love and faith very great selflessness is required. And Columba went to great lengths to overcome the pull of 'self'. We are told that 'during the night he used to have for bed, the bare rock; and for pillow, a stone ...' (III 23) But he knew that pride is an enemy too subtle to be subdued by purely physical discipline, and we catch an important glimpse of his selflessness just before his death. For many people can be very possessive about their

50

work, and take a pride in believing that they are indispensable. Not so Columba. On the evening before he died he worked at copying out the Psalms, for there were no printing presses in those days. 'And when he came to that verse ... where it is written, "But they that seek the Lord shall not want for anything that is good", he said: "Here, at the end of the page, I must stop. Let Baithene write what follows." ' (III 23)

Of course Adomnan's *Life* is full of praise for Columba. But, as we should expect of any saint, he was not universally esteemed. As Jesus said, 'Woe to you, when all men speak well of you, for so their fathers did to the false prophets.'[9] And there seem to have been a number of people—not just in the saint's early, spiritually less developed days—who hated him. Such was the unrepentant thief who 'scorned the saint; and entering his ship with the booty he scoffed at the blessed man, and mocked him.' (II 22) On another occasion someone 'rushed in with a spear, intending to kill the saint. In order to prevent this, one of the monks ... came between, ready to die for him.' (II 24) If Columba could inspire great hatred of himself, he certainly inspired the greatest love.

Columba's death and last words

We are told that 'the saint was silent for a little, as the happy latest hour drew near. Then, when the beaten bell resounded at midnight, he rose in haste and went to the church and, running, entered in advance of the others, alone; and bowing his knees in prayer he sank down beside the altar. In that moment Diormit, the attendant, following later, saw from a distance the whole church filled inside with angelic light about the saint.' Then the light faded, and the monks ran in with lamps to their dying abbot. 'The saint, whose soul had not yet departed, opened his eyes, and looked around on either side, with wonderful joy and gladness of countenance ... Then Diormit raised the holy right hand, to bless the saint's company of monks ... And after the holy benediction thus expressed he presently breathed out his

51

spirit. When that had left the tabernacle of the body, his face continued to be ruddy, and in a wonderful degree gladdened by the vision of angels, so much that it seemed like the face not of a dead man, but of a living sleeper. Meanwhile the whole church resounded with sorrowful lamentations.' (III 23)

The description of Columba's death, in full, is a most magnificent piece of writing. And his last advice is salutary. ' "I commend to you, my children, these latest words, that you shall have among yourselves mutual and unfeigned charity, with peace. If you follow this course after the example of the holy fathers, God, who gives strength to the good, will help you; and I, abiding with him, shall intercede for you. And not only will the necessaries of this life be sufficiently provided by him, but also the rewards of eternal good things will be bestowed, that are prepared for those who follow the divine commandments." ' (III 23)

A man indeed

There is a singular greatness about Columba. One not only senses powerful strength and capability, but an intense compassion coupled with genuine tenderness. He had that firm, direct approach to life that is typical of those who fully accept the reality of God's greatness and man's littleness. Hence his refreshing lack of 'beating about the bush' in religion. Thoroughly manly at all times, he acquired that profound wisdom and insight that is part and parcel of spiritual maturity.

Adomnan is of course anxious to draw our attention to the virtues of his predecessor and, in keeping with the fashion of his age, emphasizes the element of supernatural wonder. What one cannot help noticing is that experiences which most people call supernatural were, to Columba, perfectly natural. He lived in a far bigger world than most men. And before some of Adomnan's stories are dismissed out of hand as primitive inventions, or a misreading of the facts, a study should be made of some of the greatest twentieth-century

Christians. For plenty of evidence has been collected about some of our contemporaries, and near contemporaries, and very carefully scrutinized in the light of scientific knowledge. And the result of such investigations shows that life is a great deal bigger, and more wonderful, than the comparatively narrow limits of the physical sciences would lead us to expect.

But perhaps the greatest miracle of Columba's life was his own steady conversion and growth in spirit. Adomnan rather draws a veil over his hero's turbulent earlier years. But there are plenty of tales—legendary and even fabulous at times— which draw our attention to Columba's reputed original fierce temper, self-will and pugnacity. He was not necessarily welcomed by all Ireland's colonists in Argyll. And the extraordinary folk tale about him and the flounder indicates that people must have noticed an originally harsh streak in his character which accords with traditions of his early life. The violence of his passions is reflected too in the initial despair which underlies another, but quite delightful, legend in which he is said to have been cheered up after a conversation with a squirrel.

Now, whatever we may choose to make of the circumstances of all these stories—fact and fiction—what does emerge out of them is a very clearly-defined personality. And its chief characteristic is a fierce inner conflict, during which energies that could easily have been at the service of the devil, and caused diabolical harm, were harnessed to Christ. The result was one of the most attractive personalities in history. And the cost of that transformation must be known to God alone.

That the transformation was complete is clear not only from Adomnan's stories, but also from the fact that ever since then the first abbot of Iona has been known, traditionally, as 'Columba the kind'. This image persists in Gaeldom today, despite the fact that other, and perhaps equally great Christians, apparently worked over a much larger area of Scotland than was ever visited by Columba. If Adomnan, by his writing, is at all responsible for his subject's fame, at least Columba deserves his reputation.

When all is said and done, one cannot avoid the conclusion that at least one really outstanding great Christian saint lived in this northern land; that he developed a remarkably attractive personality; and that it is little wonder that he has inspired—for good—countless numbers of people ever since his own lifetime.

4 SHAKEN INTO TRUTH
The Fernaig Manuscript: men find security

Insecurity is man's common lot. And how very easily we can be reminded of this when a false sense of security is shattered.

Now what must be the most photographed building in Scotland is Eilean Donan Castle in Wester Ross. For many years during its heyday Farquhar Macrae was its constable. But he was also Vicar of Kintail for nearly fifty years during the turbulent seventeenth century, and his own sense of security was based on something far more dependable than stone walls. Turning down 'preferment' in the Lowlands, he was said to be wasting his great talents in the Highlands. His influence there was as powerful as it was benevolent, and helped—among other things—to steady a small clan whose remoteness was no defence against civil wars.

The old church of Kintail which he served may now be a ruin, but it is the hallowed burial ground of the Macraes. You can see it—Kilduich—as you cross the causeway north-wards over the waters of Loch Duich. It lies ahead of you, to the right. And often has a piper led a funeral procession there playing that very beautiful tune—and currently popular song—*Theid mi dhachaidh Chro Chinn t-Saile* (I shall go home to the fold of Kintail).

With their rich cattle pastures, surrounded by mountains and no roads, and the only sea approach guarded by a strong castle, you might think the Macraes could have led an idyllic existence. But owing largely to their close connection with the increasingly powerful Mackenzies and the latter's chiefs—the Earls of Seaforth—they not only knew what was brewing politically in Scotland and abroad, but naturally got involved in the civil wars. The Macraes were renowned as fighters, and there were not infrequently many widows in Kintail. And Farquhar Macrae knew as well as anyone else what it felt like to have one's cattle—one's livelihood—stolen by an invading army.

Duncan Macrae

Now one of his grandsons was Duncan Macrae, or Don-nachadh nam Pios, of nearby Inverinate on Loch Duich-side. He has been described as 'a remarkable man and a character pleasant to contemplate'. And the late Professor Mackinnon continues: 'I have no reason to doubt that there were many like-minded Highland gentlemen living in those days— cultured, liberal, and pious men ...' And he describes Duncan Macrae as an

> engineer and mechanician, the ardent ecclesiastic, the keen though liberal-minded politician ... the Highland chief who, among the distractions of civil war and in the scanty intervals of leisure wrested from a useful, honoured, and industrious life, sat down to compose Gaelic verse and to collect the poems composed by his countrymen and neigh-bours.'[1]

And that is his chief claim to fame when, in the late seventeenth century, he produced what is known as the *Fernaig Manuscript*. It is not only a most important document of the Gaelic language, but 'its poetry, which is mainly religious and political, affords an agreeable glimpse of the religion and the politics of the remote Highlands at the time of the Revolution.'[2] Several of the authors of the poems in this anthology were kinsmen of Duncan Macrae, though many of the compositions—a number of which are unsigned —are assumed to be by the compiler himself.

The author of the *History of the Clan Macrae* points out that the poems show that their authors

> evidently had a clear, intelligent, and comprehensive grasp of the great questions of the day ... as they affected the kingdom as a whole. Though the poems deal with the state of the country in unsettled times of warfare and revolution, they nevertheless breathe, even against political and

religious opponents, a spirit of kindly toleration which must afford . . . a pleasing contrast with the narrow bigotry and religious intolerance which formed so striking a feature of this period in the south of Scotland.[3]

Europe had just gone through one of the world's greatest 'ages of change'—that of the Renaissance–Reformation. Old ideas no longer commanded universal respect, and apparently dependable institutions had suddenly collapsed. And people were still upset and fighting when these verses were composed. Men were being forced to realize that they desperately needed some really dependable, inner stability. Some of them knew where to look for it. And not least among them was Duncan Macrae.

For us the chief value of the *Fernaig MS* lies in the fact that it shows what deeply devout Christians—mostly laymen— were thinking and feeling during a time of chronic uncertainty, unrest, and danger. The translations are reproduced here in the format of modern devotional poetry, with the use of little punctuation. Each line expresses a thought. This method may help to overcome some of the problems of translating poetry from one thought-pattern into another. And for the sake of uniformity, where necessary the English has been modernized.

The brevity and uncertainty of life

A sense of the shortness of man's life was a typical feature of the troubled sixteenth and seventeenth centuries. Western Europe was in turmoil; and civil wars are always occasions of singular bitterness, when blood relations fight on opposite sides and tear their very own country to shreds. In such conditions there is no room for complacency. Facts have to be faced. And Sir John Stewart of Appin was one who felt particularly deeply the sorrow of decay.

The world is like a deceiving cloud
like bright rays of the sun
like dew on a calm day

> or the close packed snow that is white
> the fruit of leaves on the tree
> so man's life for brevity.[4]

All those things vanish in no time. Like the fragrance of a rose or lily; the heat of summer; autumn, when all plants wither; people's joys are just as transitory. He looked around on a dying world. But what really saddened him was not the shortness of life. His 'cause of sorrow and sadness' was the thought that man could exist, and then die so soon, 'without knowledge of God's glory'.

MacCulloch of Park was Macrae's grandfather, and he too was much concerned about the same theme.

> Pity the one who prides self in the world
> when death threatens daily
> don't forget death
> remember the One who redeemed you so dearly
> when soul and body part
> your wealth does not accompany you.

So, 'don't make the world your god', but 'make God your choice'.[5] And in another poem he writes,

> Strength is for those who follow
> the way prepared for safety of soul
> from King of heaven.[6]

In a very obviously insecure world, these men had sought and found the only true security.

Duncan Macrae is very clear about his view of the world about him:

> This world is deceitful
> it constantly deceives us bitterly
> many changes there are on earth
> and many men blinded by its falsehood
> some have sold their souls
> and have changed opinion
> for the sake of gain.[7]

Here we find a man trying to put God first in all things. He did not use—abuse—his religion to buttress his politics, but very obviously tried to have 'the mind of Christ' and see life from God's point of view. His political opinions—right or wrong—were the result of this single-minded attempt. And what horrified him was the apparent dishonour of those who had changed sides in the political troubles of his day:

> It is a disgrace
> that so many have forsaken his [the king's] cause
> who were once in lowly estate
> but have now climbed by good fortune upwards.[7]

There is no self-righteousness in his complaint. One gains the vivid impression of a man of absolute integrity who is utterly horrified by 'dirty politics'. He does not therefore turn his back on public affairs, in disgust. He tries to see God's view and, as a result, is committed to one party—the one whose politics he believes are clean. That there was some good on both contending sides is no doubt easier to see now, as we look back, than it was at the time.

What made Macrae wring his hands, as it were, was his belief that political trends were contrary to God's will, and that his country was therefore courting the inevitable consequences of deliberate wrong-doing.

> Much may happen to you, O Britain
> since you refused to receive warning in time
> you do not see the cause of your fear
> for unbelief has brought disaster on you.[7]

MacCulloch warns us to beware both of obstinate people who refuse to learn God's way of goodness, and those who know his way but deliberately choose evil. He also mentions as dangerous those who—though 'wise and prudent'—never benefit their companions; and in this it sounds as if he is referring to negative people, uncommitted to life. And again there is no spirit of hatred, for he simply adds, 'pity the one who deceives himself', and, 'may the Son of God correct him.'[5]

This gospel-spirit comes as a breath of fresh air from a century that was so infected with vitriolic bitterness and rancour. Perhaps the authors of these poems were too humbly aware of their own sinfulness to become unidentified with their brother-men. Duncan Macrae writes—it would appear during a time not of special sin but of acute spiritual awareness:

> Forgive me all my sins and free me from evil
> because You know tonight my plight
> I am poor tonight
> corrupt in body
> my heart hurt
> deadly sin has wounded me.[8]

God's answer to man

MacCulloch is refreshingly clear and confident about God's answer to man's predicament.

> Let each seek growth in holiness
> at all times
> and all the good he seeks
> will come from King of heaven.[6]

How will we discover the right way to live and gain strength to follow it? By daily 'reading "the Book" [Bible] morning and evening', and by prayer. For he tells us,

> The reading and listening
> to the Gospel
> is evident to Adam's seed [descendants]
> is conducive to piety.[6]

And 'blind is he who refuses to choose' God's way.[9]

It is significant that Macrae includes in his anthology a poem each about the Creed[10], the Lord's Prayer[11], and the Ten Commandments.[12] They are unsigned and may well

have been composed by himself. And in view of God's
guidance and offered strength, he comments on Britain's ills
that,

> such conduct is unnatural
> in anyone who has received baptism
> in the name of the Trinity on high.[7]

So he prays,

> Oh! Father of grace
> do not fail us in our sore distress
> but look upon us soon with tenderness
> from your heaven above
> As You miraculously led the children of Israel
> without loss of any through the sea
> so in very deed defend Your church ...
> from the evil now fallen upon her
> It is her duty to be humble
> though she is at this moment under a cloud
> Her sins are the cause that has brought upon us harm and
>   loss
> but let us fast and mourn
> to him who went to the cross without faltering ...[7]

The authors of these poems were clear about two things.
First, the world is full of injustice; but secondly, God is just.
Therefore wrongs will inevitably be put right. And if that
doesn't happen during our lifetime, we need have no doubt
that it is most certainly going to happen in due course. So
Macrae advises,

> Let us meditate on the last day
> when it must fall to our lot to die ...
> let us meditate on what must come hereafter
> that is on the great day of judgement
> when nothing done by us in the flesh [in this world]
> can any longer be concealed.[13]

And in an unsigned poem, perhaps by him, this is emphasized:

> The quick piercing eye [of God]
> observes many changes
> nothing is done unobserved anywhere
> by the Father of light.[14]

In a long passage Macrae describes the judgement, his verse being an expansion of Christ's teaching about treating him in the least of his people. For example, the Lord says,

> For when I was thirsty and cold
> and hungry unto death in prison
> without energy or strength
> you brought true relief to my trouble ...
> your deeds of kindness towards me were not few.[13]

And the neglect of care for others brings also its inevitable reward, described by Macrae with full, terrifying biblical imagery. After all, as MacCulloch puts it,

> When they would not listen to prophets
> a law or command they did not observe
> they cannot hope for protection or help
> after despising Son of God.[15]

It is not a case of vengeance, but simply of inevitable consequence. Neglect of love leads to loss of love—in this world and the next.

A man like Duncan Macrae, who takes God seriously, is bound to be painfully aware of his own shortcomings. Any ideal of unselfish love that is worth having at all, is a standard that we have not yet reached. So he prays,

> King of the world
> who is eternal
> keep me mindful of You always
> save me from straying
> on the path of the wicked.

Guide me in the right way
King of virtues who is above
and for Jesus Your Son's sake
forgive all the sins I have committed
...
Create in me a new heart.[8]

And in another poem—as in one of John Stewart's—Macrae asks,

Increase my faith always ...
above all increase my love.[16]

God is reliable—so rejoice!
Macrae could acknowledge that

My sin has wounded me
like the burden of death,

and he prays,

Surround me till death
they [sins] have left me in suffering
may my defence at all times
be in the everlasting promise of Jesus.

The promise my King gave
who shed his blood on the cross
for all who believe shall not perish.[16]

A God who loves us so much that he can appear amongst us as a man, and die an agonizing death for us, can indeed be relied upon. No wonder that MacCulloch writes,

Let all in the world understand
the sufferings of Christ
nailed to a cross
crucified under the order of Pilate.

He suffered every pain
shed his blood to save the people

Let us ever plead
that he may be precious to us.[17]

In another poem he writes,

I shall not be disappointed.

Let me walk confidently
my desire always is for heaven
the untruthful world to forsake
and enter the way everlasting.[9]

There is a 'here and now' ring about those last lines—that
foretaste of heavenly joy that can be experienced at times by
those who try to follow Christ and forsake the selfish ideals
of sheer worldliness.

Like the Bible these poems are full of vivid black-and-white
contrasts. There is none of that dull greyness that can make
so much preaching and teaching uninspiring. Macrae and his
fellow-contributors to the *Fernaig MS* not only knew that sin
is utterly appalling, but also that God is indescribably
wonderful.

For those who have tried to follow Jesus, the final
reckoning will be a time of intense joy, writes Macrae. In
fact in his poem on the last judgement he mentions joy a
dozen times, during a great burst of praise which includes
this passage:

Oh! joyful will it be for them the while
joyful for them all that they behold
joyful to be in the city of grace
joyful to be in the presence of the judge
joyful his peace and his glory
it is not possible to declare
the greatness of the joy
of the everlasting place.[13]

And part of this joy is bound to be the contrast between
the sense of our own sinfulness, and our discovery—even here
and now—of God's incredible forgiveness. So Macrae prays,

With Your Spirit
guide me to the throne of joy
that there I may forsake
the cause of my heartache and sorrow.[16]

In an unsigned poem, probably by Macrae himself, there are some beautiful descriptions of Christ.

Just and fair
wise victorious
foster parent of the poor
Hero of dear countenance
King of numerous graces
guiding light
in every situation
the reliever of my straits ...
happy is he who knows Your love
that the world may be filled with Your love ...[14]

So MacCulloch tells us,

Every good thing to be enjoyed
comes from King of heaven
Let us first and foremost
give him the praise and glory.

At the beginning
God created the whole world
according to his will,
We should praise him
for the fruit of his labours.

We should praise God each day
and follow him
who wonderfully created man
from the dust of the earth.[6]

And that perhaps sums it all up—that God is very great, and man is very small. Only when man gets a realistic and firm grasp of that basic fact, can the sheer joy of a loving friendship with God be his to experience, for ever.

5 *STILL WATERS RUN DEEP*
George Garden's letters on Contemplative Prayer

'There was never more preaching than in this age, yet never a greater spiritual famine.' So wrote Dr George Garden, and gave his reason: 'writings and sermons . . . do not at all touch the heart.'[1]

He lived more than a hundred years after the Reformation. It was still very much an age of 'confessional religion', or enforced adherence to this or that massive and detailed statement of doctrine. It was not so much to the particular clauses of the Westminster Confession which he objected, as to the dogmatic insistence that everyone should subscribe to its 171 statements. The infinitely smaller creed, drawn up by an early council of a still united Christendom, at Nicaea, was good enough for him. And it is not unimportant to mention this; for Garden was well aware that God is to be loved by us totally—which includes our minds as well as our hearts.

But, as the late Professor Henderson has put it, 'he wished to distinguish essentials from accidentals and to insist that everything must illustrate and inculcate faith, charity, and hope', and that he recognized 'the love of God as the essence of virtue'.

Garden, who lived from 1649 to 1733, has been described as 'a leader, dignified, cultured, of strong will and determination, and at the same time lovable, deeply religious, entirely humble, and with the heart of a little child.' As a native of the north-east he went to Aberdeen University, and studied abroad. After ordination his charges included St Machar's Cathedral and the important city church of St Nicholas. A change of government and religion led to Garden being deprived. And from then on, though occasionally visiting London and the Continent, he chiefly lived quietly in Aberdeen, ministering in a small oratory, in his home where his sister kept house. For a time he lived in what appears to have been a monastic community founded by him at Rosehearty, but about which we unfortunately know almost nothing.

In a pamphlet, hostile to Garden's views, he was described as 'an able preacher, one who teacheth the truth in sincerity, without respect of persons'. And another antagonist described him as 'a known pattern of piety ... all that reading and knowledge he is master of'. 'As to Garden's high character there is universal agreement' wrote Professor Henderson; and he described him as 'a keen missionary, who was himself the best argument for his views'.

Judging by his quotations he was steeped both in Scripture and also in the spiritual classics. Anyone with the slightest familiarity with the Bible will recognize long passages of Garden's letters to be, in reality, a series of scriptural texts deftly woven together in order to draw his reader's attention to one or other of God's glories. His quotations from Christian writers down the ages range from Augustine and Bernard, to John of the Cross and Francis de Sales—to mention only a few.

Was it not an appalling waste of God's gifts to deprive such a man of a leading position in one of Scotland's chief cities? For Garden's views—powerfully backed by his respected character and learning—not only upset a Presbyterian General Assembly, but also prevented him from being offered an Episcopalian bishopric. One can see their point. Some novel views were being published on the Continent, and Garden's wide contacts enabled him to study them and to see what was good in them. He was accused of accepting the bad with the good. There is no need for us here to examine this short-lived controversy. It is only mentioned in order to show why Garden lived for years an apparently retired and obscure life.

God works in a mysterious way. With hindsight we can see that Garden was being deliberately removed from the public life of the Church, which is ever in danger of super-

67

ficiality. All his energies were gradually fused and concentrated in one direction, like a laser-beam. For love,
focused and intensified in prayer, penetrates the heart. And
out of those obscure years of inevitable suffering known to
God alone—and occasional joys undreamt of by the world—
emerged his letters on contemplative prayer. They were
written largely to a circle of devout laymen in the north-east
and elsewhere; and we shall now examine two of his very
long ones. These were written to James Cunningham of Barns
in Fife, in 1709 and 1710.[2]

To James Cunningham

With typical humility Garden writes hoping 'that something
may be written here which may work together for your good'.
And, considering God's greatness he advises 'an entire
resignation of your own will, opinions, reason, affections, and
all unto him. This is the very essence of all religion and the
true way to real divine experimental knowledge.'

To expect such knowledge without committal is im-
pertinent, but very popular these days. Anyway, Garden
continues and describes the result of such committal:

> Such a pure love of God, and of your neighbours for his
> sake, such a profound humility and deep sense of your own
> nothingness, such an abandoning of your will, and an
> entire resignation of all you are and all you have to his
> will; such a contentedness and satisfaction to suffer
> reproach or any other evil for his sake, and in obedience
> to what you are persuaded to be his will; such an absolute
> and unlimited faith in God so that he is become all in all
> to you, can be effected by nothing but the Spirit of God;
> for the fruits of the Spirit are love, joy, peace, long-
> suffering, gentleness, goodness, faith, meekness, tem-
> perance. And all this being the fruit of that silent prayer
> and pure faith in God which you are now led into, and
> which, as you know, so many spiritual souls have recom-
> mended from their own practice ...

In these days when so much emphasis is often placed on techniques of praying, Garden plainly states that 'the promises made are not to this way of prayer in particular, but to the seeking of God with the whole heart'. As the handling of our desires and affections is vital, he continues, 'we are bid not only to pray, but to watch that we enter not into temptation.'

Next comes a necessary warning.

They who give themselves to the prayer of silence, it is supposed that their senses, appetites, and passions are already in a great measure mortified and subdued, and that the soul has already acquired the habits of virtues, and has a will habitually prompt to be humble, obedient, poor in spirit, and virtuous in all things, also [i.e. otherwise] they may be led into a false quiet which does not purify the heart but exposes it to delusion.

Contemplative Prayer

The prayer of silence being the soul's turning away the understanding from all the creatures and all their images and the fixing it by pure faith on God the supreme truth and good, as he is in himself infinitely beyond the conceptions of any creature, and by ardently loving that supreme and boundless and incomprehensible loveliness, the great end of this is to be rooted and grounded in divine hope and love, and in all virtue, and while it is exercised only for this end, it cannot but be of excellent profit to the soul, and there is no occasion of deceit in this.

For modern readers it is often necessary to add that this is not a matter of religious experiences, the desire for which can be simply selfish. Following his advice about virtue, Garden continues, 'he who prays in this manner does not wait for speeches, nor motions, nor extraordinary lights, nor other miracles; nor desires any other thing but always most profoundly and firmly to believe in God, to hope in him and

69

to love him in time and throughout unchangeable eternity.'
Religious experiences may of course come, unsought.

But if such souls have at any time extraordinary lights and
conditions about particular things, they are not wedded to
them, because they know that what is known, possessed,
and felt here below is not God; who here on earth has
given himself to be believed, not understood; hoped for, not
possessed; and loved, not felt.

For such a person 'clouds and darkness are round about
him'. That is the normal condition. The soul

is placed as in a dry and thirsty land where no water is:
and yet it does still more hunger and thirst after God
and prayer, and its disgust of temporal things increases the
more, while it seems to itself to have no virtue and not
to love God. And this is its true purification, not merely
from the images, and the love of bodily things, but from
self, self-love, self-complacency, self-seeking, or the
cleaving to anything but God.

Nothing at this stage brings consolation. What is happening?
Garden explains: 'our heavenly Father ... is pleased ... to
wean your heart more effectually from self and all creatures,
it is for your good ...'

God is a Spirit, and communicates himself to the soul in a
spiritual manner; and if the notices he gives the soul be
when it is still and free from all imaginations ... one would
be apt to think that this would be manifested in the still
and small voice, and not by such agitations of the body,
as appear in the prophets of the present age which one
should think would rather pull the soul out of its silent
state, than preserve it in it. This was not the way that our
Lord spoke, who had the Spirit without measure.

Warfare with evil

'The gospel of Jesus Christ even though preached through strife, if it be received in an honest heart, the Spirit of God may there bring forth good fruit . . .' That remark of Garden's reminds one perhaps especially of those simple devout souls one meets in every denomination. And he goes on to describe the various strategies of Satan against the Church through the ages, stating that

> he first stirred up all the powers of the world against Christianity to suppress and stifle it in its birth. When it flourished the more by persecution then he set up to be a Christian, brought in all his followers and all the power of wealth of the world into the Church, and his adherents into the most eminent places in it, and appeared highly zealous for the outside of Christianity, undermining in the meantime its true inward life and spirit. When this corruption was come to its height, and many serious persons groaned for a reformation of life and manners, he then set up for a reformer, and divides the Christian world into a great many contending parties, fills them with strife and envy against one another, and so with confusion and every evil work, and makes them place their religion in a zeal against the errors and corruptions of the contrary parties, without taking care to deny themselves and to be followers of Jesus in humility and charity. And when the Spirit of God begins in the several parties of Christendom to open men's eyes, to let them see the folly and madness of their mutual strife and contention about the outward rights, forms, and opinions among Christians, and to awaken them to the more inward life and spirit of Christianity by learning to take off their heart, love, and desires from self and earthly things, and to turn them wholly unto God; Satan then sets up to be a mystic and an inward spiritual person . . .

What then are we to do against these wiles? He tells us:

continue to ask wisdom of God in all sincerity, and he will direct you. Let us labour to be the true followers of Jesus Christ, in the spirit of penitence, selfdenial, humility, and charity without respect to any party, and live in the midst of parties without being of a party. We are called to be the followers of our Lord Jesus Christ, and not either of [he mentions several denominational founders] ... This is one true shepherd who calls us to one sheepfold. Let us hear his voice and follow him ... We have one great enemy and that is self, and if that were subdued, nothing could hurt us. May we deny our selves and take up the cross and follow Jesus ... By this let it be known that we are the disciples of Jesus that we love one another.

Having read this last paragraph we might well remind ourselves that Garden could have remained in charge of St Nicholas' Church, Aberdeen, if he had been prepared to compromise his principles. His own life is an interesting study in the relationship between truth and charity. His own vision of God enabled him to grasp the wholeness of life, where so many of the rest of us can only see it in fragments.

Encouragements and warnings

In his second letter Garden returns to emphasize again that contemplative prayer is not a matter of technique, but is about giving one's life totally to Christ. He writes,

'how can it be imagined that God will communicate his light and Spirit to a soul that follows its own will and desires, only because at certain times it suspends the acting of its faculties, waiting for the divine communication, and gives itself to the prayer of silence?'

If we don't yet feel ready to give ourselves totally, then he encourages us to do our best.

Neither must you think that what I have said respects any sincere soul who desires to seek God with its whole heart, and yet having strong corruptions to mortify and subdue, against which it wrestles, it is often foiled, yet is not thereby discouraged, but in the strength of the divine grace goes on to resist them, being confident that God will at last give it the victory. Such if they happen in the exercise of this to fall into delusion, it is to be hoped that it is for their trial, and that God will afterwards discover [i.e. show] it to them.

He then warns us against creating false religious experiences ourselves.

And yet they may by this way of the internal silence of their faculties kindle a fire within and compass themselves about with their own sparks, and walk in the light of their own fire, and in the sparks that they have kindled, and take all for divine light, and divine communications, and possess the minds of sincere persons with the same persuasion concerning them.

Years before modern psychology Garden was distinguishing various sources of experience. He wrote of religious experiences that 'though these may sometimes be motions from the divine grace, yet such may also proceed from the motions of one's own mind, and understanding, or from the delusion of a foreign spirit, and yet be looked upon as divine motions.' So great and humble dependence upon God is needed. He writes:

and therefore it is our duty to apply to the Father of lights, and beg that he may vouchsafe us his Spirit, and grant us such light and direction as is agreeable to his will, but we must not presently conclude that every inward conviction we receive upon our interior recollection is an infallible light.... And though the chief duty of the blind man is to have faith in God, and to depend upon his good providence for his preservation, yet he must do this, not in trusting to his own eyes, but in submitting to the conduct and direction of an honest faithful guide, who sees the light and knows the way ... The true answer and operation of

73

the Holy Spirit in this state is to direct us to the Holy Rule of Christian life and doctrine, and (we being blind ourselves) to follow the conduct of him who had the Spirit without measure ... in the humble prayer of faith [we] will listen to the counsel and advices of those who have been immediately directed by the Holy Spirit of God, but especially and above all to Jesus Christ himself ... And therefore instead of aspiring after inward divine infallible light in my present corrupt state, I am moved to live by faith and not by sight, and to make the life and doctrine of Jesus my rule, my meditation, and my practice.

Although we must be humble enough to be ready to take advice, Garden issues a warning: 'our Saviour bids us beware of false prophets, ... he tells us, by their fruits we shall know them,' and then goes on to point out, 'if the prophets, of whom our Lord warns us had not apparently good fruits, how should the elect be in hazard of being deceived by them?' And he warns us about the necessary, though charitable use, of our critical faculty, that 'seeing such apparent signs and miracles' in false prophets there are people who 'will be afraid lest they should offend God, if they should believe any evil of persons so wonderful for their goodness and virtue.' Human nature can be very gullible.

False negative quiet

Some contemporary popular 'methods of meditation' set about, by self-hypnosis or other means, to make the mind a blank. No doubt those who practise this kind of thing feel some refreshment afterwards. But it is not Christian prayer—whether meditation or contemplation. Garden writes of those who simply 'rid themselves of all images and acts. But a soul that loves God cannot embrace this quiet, for the love of God, and an inward touch of the divine grace is not idle.'

'Now this divine light is', he says, 'the eternal Word,' and 'our state here is to walk by faith, and not by light ... Our great duty is to consult Jesus, God-man, his life and doctrine.

"Go," says he, "and teach them to do all things that I have commanded you." He does not say, Go, and teach them to consult only the light within them ... But here is the true standard whereby to judge whether the inward light to which men pretend, be divine or not. Jesus, he is the light of the world, if we follow him, we shall not walk in darkness, but shall have the light of life.' And all this is vital, 'for the establishment of truth, unity, and peace, there must be a general known standard whereby all sentiments, motions, and lights pretended to be from God, ought to be measured.'

George Garden does not rank among the world's famous teachers of prayer. But that, perhaps, is one of his attractions. He was simply a man who wanted, with all his being, a genuine, real, authentic relationship with God. Judging by available evidence, he used all he had—heart, mind, and body—to achieve just that. And he seems to have been remarkably successful. For through Jesus he approached the invisible Godhead; and those who knew him saw in him clearly something of the sheer attractiveness of the Holy Spirit. When his advice was asked about the things of God, he wrote at length out of his own first-hand experience. For his quoting of famous writers comes as from someone who has discovered for himself the truth of their teaching. Many of these things—elementary as they may be—need to be repeated for the benefit of every generation; and perhaps never more so than in our own confused times.

N.B.
The reference to Garden's ejection from his church post on political grounds is open to question. Historians are now laying much greater emphasis on the religious motives of many of those who were Jacobite in politics.

6 BEYOND THE MOUNTAINS
Richard of St-Victor: studies in prayer-life

He 'must love Jesus, and Jesus alone.'[1] So has been summarized the essence of the life of a Canon Regular. These men
were not similar to cathedral canons today; for they were
monks, but their rule permitted a certain amount of active
evangelism. Like the monk—in the proper sense of that word
—their contribution to Church life was especially to reflect
the Christ of the wilderness, and his whole nights in prayer.
But Canons Regular also on occasion would go out to preach.
In fact from the writings of Adam of Dryburgh—on the
Borders—we catch a vivid glimpse of one of their stricter
communities. They simply attempted to live out very literally
the corporate life as described in the Acts of the Apostles. And
in the twelfth century this movement was in its prime, fired by
ideals of simplicity and humility in a life of total dedication to
loving God and one's neighbour, and expressing this
chiefly—but not exclusively—in the hidden warfare of
prayer.

Now during that century another Scotsman, Richard,
went to Paris and joined a similar type of community at St-
Victor. This French abbey was then at the height of its fame
for spiritual vitality, and Richard became its prior, or next 'in
command' to the abbot himself. If the young Scot had ever
thought that freedom from worldly cares would spell a life of
bliss he would soon have been disillusioned. In close-knit
community life the problems of human relationships are
intensified. There's no escape. Nor can refuge be taken in
worldly consolations. And after a most unfortunate choice of
abbot, prior Richard found himself caught between the
upper and nether millstones of a superior on the one hand,
and a community on the other that would naturally seek his
support. That abbot in fact represented the very opposite of

the ideal of simplicity and humility among brothers for whom he bore responsibility. He was so bad that eventually he was deposed by the Pope. And in 1173 Richard, still young, died.

That is virtually all that is known about him—apart from his writings. But the latter gained him an eminent reputation amongst writers on Christian spirituality in the West, where he pioneered a systematic and psychological approach to the experience of prayer. He fused the mystical traditions of eastern and western Christendom, being able to see both as part of a coherent whole—or perhaps we should say that he recognized each as saying the same thing in a slightly different way. In this lay his genius. And one commentator has stated that in his search for truth he arrived at 'the ultimate truth, namely that God is love', and that 'he is always alive with wonder and admiration, gratitude, and joy'.[2]

Now that is exactly what we should expect from contemplating God, the ultimate good. And Richard's concern is not so much to classify human experience, but to help people to progress in their own contemplation of God. In his method he is remarkably 'modern', for he follows the principle of starting with ordinary human experiences, and then leading his readers on. From human love he progresses to divine love. And all with the purpose of encouraging others to persevere. Hence his emphasis is laid far more on the joys of the hidden life with God than on those inevitable, purifying trials, that every sinful human being must also experience if he is to be fit to enjoy a loving friendship with his Creator.

In this study of Richard's teaching we shall try as far as possible to let him speak for himself. The few notes between quotations are not attempts to summarize unquoted passages, but are an attempt to help modern readers to understand the subject. Many people know much of this teaching from their own experience, but are quite unused to seeing it described in this way. We often need an experienced Christian to point out how this teaching and our own experience (often apparently quite ordinary) connect.

We can have many experiences at an elementary level. If we co-operate with God we can go through the same experiences later at a deeper level. But God has many ways of training us to turn away from our selfish selves and find our true fulfilment in him. And writings on prayer, or friendship with God, are of great value if they can help us to understand what God is doing. For that understanding—which is done intuitively by the heart rather than by the head—should enable us all the better to co-operate with him.

Prayer is love

At the beginning of the first of his writings which we shall consider Richard goes straight to the point:[3] 'Love urges me to speak of love.' And typically he starts with human affection.

> For there is affection for mankind, for the group, for kindred and family, and the brotherhood and so forth and many more kinds in this world. But above all these degrees there is that ardent and burning love which penetrates the heart, inflames the affection and transfixes the soul itself to the very core, so that she may truly say: 'I am wounded by love.' Let us consider what this surpassing quality of Christ's love is . . .

He then continues to encourage us. 'Whatever offers itself . . . is quickly rejected and immediately despised, if it does not foster this love nor serve this desire.' At once we recognize that prayer is not only a matter of the heart but of the head too, and Richard teaches that 'in spiritual things, however, we always love first by deliberation rather than affection.' So, 'if we wish to love with all our desire, let all our thoughts be on this, all our deliberation and all our meditation.' And then the warning: 'But if we have an affection for something which we do not love for God's sake, the adulterous affection immediately breaks the constancy of the highest charity and diminishes its strength in proportion as it draws or drives the soul to extraneous desires . . .'

Singlemindedness must develop. 'In the first degree the soul thirsts for God, in the second she thirsts to go to God, in the third she thirsts to be in God, in the fourth she thirsts in God's way.' And he describes the last degree as being the stage when not 'in temporal matters only but also in spiritual things, the soul reserves nothing for her own will but commits all things to God, never thinking about herself but about the things of Jesus Christ ...' The four degrees are then summarized:

> In the first she enters in by meditation, in the second she ascends by contemplation, in the third she is led into jubilation, in the fourth she goes out by compassion. In the first degree a spiritual feeling sweeter than honey enters into her soul ... This is that spiritual sweetness and inward delight which is the milk and food of those who are as newborn babes ...

A milk diet doesn't go on for growing children. 'In this same state the soul is led by God into the wilderness,' and Richard makes a parallel here between the soul's experience and that of the Hebrews led into the wilderness during the Exodus. 'But first we must leave Egypt behind ...' and 'suffer famine'. If this is tough,

> truly the more fully the love of God overcomes any other affection, the more often and more abundantly it refreshes the soul with inward gladness. In this state the mind sucks honey from the stone and oil from the hardest rock ... In this state the Lord often descends from heaven and visits him who sits in darkness and the shadow of death ... Nevertheless he reveals his presence but without showing his face ... His loveliness is felt but his form is not discerned.'

Why these consolations? They are, Richard tells us, 'to give her greater courage', for we are being trained to live not in our own strength, but in God's.

As we progress Richard describes the joy of intimacy.

In this state it [the soul] is wholly subdued, the host of carnal desires are deeply asleep and there is silence in heaven ... And any suffering that is left is absorbed in glory ... then it sheds its very self altogether and puts on that divine life, and being wholly conformed to the beauty it has seen, passes wholly into that glory.

But this state is only possible for those who are prepared to learn to become selfless love, with all the suffering that that entails.

When in this way the soul has been reduced in the divine fire, softened to the very core and wholly melted, nothing is wanting except that she should be shown what is God's goodwill ... And as liquefied metal runs down easily wherever a passage is opened, so the soul humbles herself spontaneously to be obedient in this way ... This is the form of the humility of Christ to which every man must conform himself, who desires to attain to the highest degree of perfect charity. For greater love has no man than this, that a man lay down his life for his friends.

How do we start?

In what does the battle of life consist? Richard tells us[4] that 'the affection of the soul is not withdrawn from illicit things and set upon right things without great labour'. So how do we start?—'he who thinks of the Lord in goodness discerns him who is the beginning of all things ... So the imagination is always ready and in all things, and the reason can make use of its servant everywhere.'

But this 'servant' needs controlling, for 'when we are saying psalms or praying, though we would shut out phantasies of thought or the images of things from the eyes of our heart, we are unable to do so.' This reminds us that we need God. 'And therefore the Holy Spirit is called Paraclete which means comforter, for often and gladly he comforts the soul that is humbled with tears of penitence ...'

When that begins to happen 'from now on a certain

fellowship begins to exist between God and the soul and friendship is established so that the soul often feels she is being visited by God and she is not only comforted by his coming but at times filled with ineffable joy.' And 'not only God's generosity but also our sin, commends his goodness to us.' This, Richard tells us, 'is the first road towards contemplation of invisible things for a beginner.'

As usual he is thoroughly grounded in the Bible. 'We must not overlook the fact that the Sacred Scriptures make use of this way of thinking and condescend to human infirmity. For they describe unseen things by the form of visible things and impress them upon our memories by the beauty of desirable forms.' This of course places great emphasis on our thinking. 'Most men blame themselves for perverse deeds or wicked desires, but very few condemn themselves because of disordered thoughts.' This is serious, for 'those who put their trust in false and deceptive goods cannot find the real good ...' And 'the human mind cannot arrive at true joy except by abstinence and patience. He who would have this joy must exclude both false pleasures and vain anxiety ... For we know that a mind fluctuating among many desires, troubled by tempest is not to be admitted to that interior joy ...' That joy 'is that truly blessed country, namely the tranquil stability of the mind, when it is wholly recollected into itself and fixed unmoving in the one desire for eternity.' So Richard adds, 'Woe is me a wretched man, for to this day I live a wanderer and exile upon this earth; wandering about following my desires, an exile experiencing wretchedness.'

All this however can be turned to good use. 'The more we are harassed by bitter temptation and exercised by frequent dangers the more perfectly shall we learn discretion, and often where we fail in other virtues we gain in discretion.' Thus 'the soul is carefully taught and eventually it is brought to full self-knowledge' for 'in vain does the eye of the heart which is not yet fit to see itself, try to see God.' So, 'let him who desires to see God wipe his mirror and cleanse his heart.'

81

Once more we are reminded, through our efforts, of our total dependence upon God. 'For never does the mind attain to this grace by its own activity. This gift is from God and not of man's deserving. But certainly no one ever receives such a great grace without tremendous labour and burning desire.' We have to prepare ourselves for God's gifts, and not just sit back expecting them to drop out of heaven. When a person by desire and humility is ready, Richard describes the effect of God's gift of contemplation:

> For when the mind of man is carried beyond itself all the limits of human reasoning are overpassed. For the whole system of human reasoning succumbs to that which the soul perceives of the divine light, when she is raised above herself and ravished in ecstasy ... for when the mind is carried away in contemplation it experiences how inadequate is human reason ... What did Aristotle or Plato find or the host of philosophers, compared with this?

And, as usual, Richard again turns to the Bible. 'Do you not see that nothing but the truth leads one to this mountain and guides one up?' he asks. And then adds that Christ is 'the way, the truth, and the life.'

The story of the transfiguration is next used to illustrate our theme. 'Lest the labour of the way terrify you or the difficulty of the ascent make you draw back, listen and attend to what the fruit of victory will be' he writes. 'On the peak of this mountain Jesus is transfigured; there too Moses and Elias are seen and both are recognized without a sign, and there too the voice of the Father to the Son is heard. Are not all of these wonderful and to be desired?' Why then do relatively few experience them? He tells us: 'Oh how many we find today who are industrious in reading but lazy at work, tepid in prayer, presuming nevertheless that they are able to reach the heights of this mountain. But when will those who are not led by Christ learn?'

We must not hide the fact that many believe they have

reached the top of this mountain when it is apparent that they have only come to the foothills . . . For that glory of the divine wisdom which is seen from the extreme height of contemplation, cannot be described in any way by the experience of the human faculties . . . So long, then, as you delay in the valley and do not ascend on high, Christ teaches you only about the lower things that belong to the earth.

'But . . . if you feel you have seen Christ transfigured, do not believe too easily whatever you may see in him, or hear from him unless Moses and Elias are with him.' Why? For 'I suspect every truth which is not confirmed by the authority of Scripture . . . You see therefore, that both are transfigured, Christ and the devil, but Christ confirms the truth of his light by two witnesses.'

In all matters of 'religious experience' it is important to seek reliable advice. One very rough and ready rule of thumb is that any experience which puffs one up with pride comes from the devil, and an experience which is humbling may well come from God. Richard's emphasis on testing everything by the Bible reminds one of Christ's own replies during his temptation in the wilderness. He certainly knew his Bible and so should we.

God veils his presence because sinful human beings are not able to bear the sight of his glory. Hence even the partial revealing of his presence can be terrifying. As Richard reminds us,

as soon as the thunder of the Father's voice is heard the disciples fall to the ground. They who hear fall down at the thunder of the divine voice because the power of the human mind fails in the presence of that which is divinely inspired and unless it leaves the narrow limits of human reasoning, the depth of the intelligence cannot expand to take in the secrets of the divine inspiration.

Prayer embraces the whole of life

True knowledge, love, and goodness are therefore all linked. So Richard asks,[5] 'Would any man doubt that sanctification includes the cleansing of a man from his uncleanness and the purgation of his mind from all malice and wickedness? For a man is defiled by these things. He is purified by wisdom ...' How then does he gain this? Richard replies by asking,

> Yet what is that best part that Mary chose but to wait and taste how sweet the Lord is? ... This is the work which will never come to an end in time or eternity. For the contemplation of truth begins in this life but is carried on perpetually in the next. By the contemplation of truth man is instructed unto righteousness and prepared for glory ... Truly nothing else so purifies the heart of all worldly affection, nothing inflames the soul more with heavenly love.

So, 'learn to be at rest, not only from evil works but also from idle thoughts ... do what the Psalmist teaches: "Be still and know that I am God." '

Most people start with meditation and go on to contemplation, but these days rational meditation is not infrequently by-passed. Richard's distinction is therefore not unimportant. He says,

> thinking, slow-footed, wanders hither and thither along bypaths, caring not where they will lead. Meditation with great mental industry, plods along the steep and laborious road keeping the end in view. Contemplation on a free wing, circles around with great nimbleness wherever the impulse takes it.

The first two occupations are man-made; the last is God's gift. In the first it is like the flapping of a bird's wings. Then, when the bird has gained height the wind lifts it and it soars. Richard describes further: 'Contemplation abides untoiling and fruitful. Thinking roams about, meditation investigates, contemplation wonders ... Thinking moves from one thing to another rambling aimlessly. Meditation is perseveringly intent on one thing only. Contemplation sheds the light of a single ray upon innumerable objects.' Again he makes the distinction that meditation 'is an industrious attention of the mind concentrated diligently upon the investigation of some object', while 'contemplation is a free and clear vision of the mind fixed upon the manifestation of wisdom in suspended wonder'. What a magnificent description! And what a world of difference there is between ecclesiastical pronouncements that emerge from mere human intellect, and those that well up out of the depths of contemplation.

People who have been taught meditation but are being led on to contemplation usually go through a period of feeling 'at sea'. Richard remarks:

> For when a truth has been long sought, and is at last discovered, the mind usually receives it greedily, wonders at it with exultation and for a long time rests therein in wonder. And this already shows meditation exceeding its bounds and passing over into contemplation.

Richard then goes on to describe methods of discovering things.

> We learn the meaning of white and black, hot and cold, sweet and bitter by the bodily sense, we do not prove them by reasoning. True and false, just and unjust, useful and useless, these we discern by reason and not by any bodily sense. That God is of one substance in three persons, is not taught us by any bodily sense, nor can we be convinced of it by any human reasoning ... we often prove a thing by authority and confirm it by arguments and convince by analogies, yet our intelligence does not fully understand even when the thing is proved and we are persuaded.

85

(By 'intelligence' Richard means intellectual intuition rather than intellectual reasoning—which is a more shallow process.) So true 'knowledge is given to the prophetic man by a multitude of divers revelations'. And 'to the faithful mind when it is supported by such help, many reasons suggest themselves from every side, many arguments present themselves to help her in her investigations ...' All of which is perfectly natural.

> For the perfection of knowledge is to know God and the fullness of this knowledge is the fullness of glory, the perfection of grace and eternity of life. 'For this', he [Christ] says, 'is eternal life, to know thee the true God, and Jesus Christ whom thou hast sent.'

Richard returns to the theme of purity of heart.

> For we know that the depth of the heart is better purged, the purity of the mind restored, clouds of obscurity cleared away, the heart's serenity more quickly and more completely brought about by true contrition of heart, by deep and inward spiritual sorrow, than by any other means ... By this our conception of the love and fear of God must be tempered, lest the soul, softened by too great reliance on divine forgiveness melts into weakness, or by an unbalanced conception of the divine severity, grows hardened by despair ...

This is all most important, for 'to behold the wonders of the majesty of God' asks Richard, 'who is fit for this?' And he goes on, 'I think that nobody, nobody at all I say, among rational beings, is free from the love of his own excellence ... unless he is really able to despise himself in comparison with the things of which we have spoken.' And then he makes a comparison: 'Truly when birds want to fly they unfold their wings. So truly, we also must extend the wings of our hearts by desire and await the time of the divine showing at every hour and moment ...'

We are to live, and go about our business, in fact, as those

86

who 'wait upon the Lord'. Thus our horizon will expand. As Richard says, 'we must not only raise our minds to that which we may have in this life but also consider that vision of divine contemplation which we hope for in the world to come . . .' There is no selfishness about this. Quite the reverse. 'For love arising from knowledge and knowledge coming from love must always grow in us . . .'

Courage

To bare one's soul and meet God face to face is naturally funked by mortal man. So Richard states, 'How many there are who think themselves ready and yet at the moment of visitation tremble with fear . . .' We need courage indeed. The fire of God's love begins to burn out our self-esteem when we accept him into the heart of our lives. To learn true security we need to lose worldly self-confidence. So we are told, about Christ,

> always be prompt and prepared to receive the friend who knocks, without giving offence by delay . . . For indeed it is a strange kind of love that does not welcome the spouse nor admit the friend. Therefore first see to it that you are ready to throw out the crowds of noisy people when he begins to knock . . . All thoughts whether vain or evil are to be considered extraneous, for none of them is of any use to us.

So,

> cast out the whole crowd, not only the thoughts but also the affections, so that we may cling to the embraces of our beloved with greater freedom and thus with greater joy . . . He is seen by contemplation, until at the sight of this un-expected vision and in wonder at his beauty, the soul grows warm, burns more and more and at last is wholly enflamed until she is altogether reformed unto true purity and in-ward beauty . . . She sees herself alone with the beloved, when having forgotten all outward things, she directs her

desire away from herself, into the love of her beloved ...
and the thought of both the good and the evil she has done
causes her to break into thanksgiving and then offer sacrifices of deep devotion both for the graces received and for
the pardon vouchsafed.

Consider what it is in your life that you have loved most
dearly, desired most anxiously; what made you most glad
and pleased you above all things. And now consider
whether you feel that violence of affection, and fullness of
pleasure when you burn with desire for the greatest Lover
and when you rest in his love? ... Truly if we can be comforted or derive gladness from any outward thing whatever, I venture to assert that our beloved does not yet
occupy the ultimate depths of passionate love.

This does not refer simply to pleasure, but fully satisfying consolation; and perhaps the most common first awareness of this
is at the time of bereavement, when many a Christian has
learnt that no human consolation suffices, but only Christ's.
Once that lesson has been learnt, what Richard is teaching
can be grasped all the more readily.

Our business then is to wait on God, ready and receptive.
As Moses waited on Mount Horeb so we must

wait in the mount while with great labour and mental
effort we accustom ourselves to abide for a long time in this
high state. But at last we come to the seventh day when this
laborious uplifting of the mind is changed into delight, and
the mind rises up without effort.

Afterwards, 'though we may remember something of this experience ... we are not able to understand or remember the
manner of our seeing nor the nature of the vision ... for every
effort of ours is made by grace alone.' At a deep level the
lesson—whatever it may be—has of course been learnt; so
there is no need to memorize the method of our learning it.
Once again Richard takes his analogies from Moses, and
from the transfiguration, when he writes, 'this entering into

the cloud, does it not mean that going forth of the mind out of itself and the darkening of the mind from its memory of surrounding things?'

> The human soul is led up above herself by wonder, when radiant with infused heavenly light and lost in wonder at the supreme beauty of God, she is torn from the foundation of her being. Like flashing lightning, the deeper she is cast down in self-depreciation in the face of the beauty she sees, so much the higher and the more rapidly does she rebound in her desire for the highest, and carried away above herself, she is lifted up to the heavens.

And once again, as so often in spiritual writings, comes the analogy of the desert; for 'unless it be lifted up above itself the mind will not be carried away into ecstasy, unless it desert itself altogether . . .' This is of course the whole purpose of Christian asceticism—to co-operate with the Holy Spirit by not pandering to our self-centred 'self'. And God usually gives us plenty of opportunities in ordinary daily life to deny this 'self'.

If we develop a 'greatness of wonder' towards God, what will happen? Richard tells us that 'the mind therefore rises up like the dawn' and 'while thus growing it at last transcends the limits of human capacity'. And if all this seems quite beyond normal Christian experience, he writes encouragingly: 'let us note that the splendour of that divine showing sometimes . . . rouses the indolent or wakens the sleeper'. But in whatever ways God chooses to train us, Richard says the path will lie through meditation, then contemplation, and finally ecstasy of wonder. If God gives us a foretaste of a stage ahead, it will be simply to encourage us.

Humbling experiences will be sent to curb pride. And Richard tells us that

> often, after many signs of its progress, the mind of man is attacked by insistent and importunate temptations, fiercely shaken and cast down from the sublime height of

89

its security and tranquillity, lest it should miserably and foolishly glory in its own fortitude under a continuous sequence of struggles.

True joy

Anyone who has ever experienced anything of the joy of Christ, especially when its genuineness is tested by a lack of any earthly happiness at the time, will know that there is no joy like it. So Richard states quite plainly that 'unbelievers . . . cannot possess joy in any way . . .' He also says that 'we cannot have these delights continually in this mere earthly life'. And he reiterates a warning—so necessary for some people in particular:

let nobody presume upon his own powers for such exalta-
tion or uplifting of the heart or ascribe it to his own merits. For it is certain that this comes not from human deserving but is a divine gift . . . Therefore she is compelled to expect and to go on expecting while her desire is often deferred greatly and for long, while she can neither have her de- lights at will nor refrain her soul from these desires.

Nevertheless when one who has arrived at this grace and feels it to be taken away from him more than is usual . . the soul must . . recall the gifts of the divine goodness to the eye of memory, and by such recollection move itself to deep and devout thanksgiving.

(In this respect the keeping of a 'spiritual diary', with special emphasis on blessings received, can be of the greatest value. One cannot always trust one's memory.)

In a very deep sense when we are alone we are closer to other people. Not only does the 'communion of saints' take on a new dimension, but we are linked, intimately through Christ, with everyone. And so it may be fitting to end these extracts from writings on the most personal kind of prayer on a corporate note. Richard says, 'By psalmody and praise we prepare the way of the Lord by which he vouchsafes to come to us and to reveal to us something of his wondrous mysteries.'

7 WITH GOD IN THE WILDERNESS
as described in a traditional Gaelic poem

Collecting the traditional poetry of the Highlands and Islands became the life-work of Alexander Carmichael. Not least owing to the prolonged onslaught on Gaelic culture, during the last century the use of these prayers and other verses was already on the decline. They had been said or chanted to accompany almost every daily activity probably from time immemorial. Some are thought to have originated as early as Christianity itself in Scotland.

Now Dr Carmichael sub-titled his collection 'hymns and incantations', and one section is simply headed 'charms'. And not a few of the poems, by the nineteenth century at least, had been placed in the context of folk-tales of varying worth. As a result, the ordinary reader will very likely overlook the genuine Christian material in this vast anthology. A verse, described as a charm, may have been used—or abused—in this way by Carmichael's time. When examined on its own merits it may not infrequently be found to be a piece of genuine Christian devotion, no doubt originally composed and used as a prayer.

Similarly one can wonder how some of the poetry ever became attached to the story from which it is said to have originated. And this is especially true of the following composition.[1] We shall therefore examine it purely on its own merits.

The originator of these verses is lost—in more senses than one—in the mountains. We shall think of the lover who finds her as Christ our divine lover. And in the light of Christian experience try to grasp something of the inner meaning of this poem.

My lover found me in my sleep,
  I wearying for his coming;
I crouching beneath rough rocks,
  Oh King! how shameful the condition.

To be weary of life is really to be weary of death—of an existence that has no real worth-while purpose about it. It has no point, so why go on? Most people have a desire to hide from some of life's experiences at least, wishing to escape them. When God offers so many opportunities to become really alive, it is shameful to hide in one's shell, behind the barriers of an artificial mask and unnecessary reserve. Withholding outgoing love, and not developing the person we really are, should lead to our longing for someone to pull us out of our shell.

I without understanding or reason,
  Oh King! tearful was the awaking;
That grace for which I seek,
  'Tis a breath of the Spirit of prayer.

To overcome this false kind of existence there must be the moment of truth—the facing the fact of our trying to hide. Knowledge of the reality can be painful indeed. Yet we have in us the spark of the divine. It must be stirred up. And prayer is God praying within us. He is as close as that.

It was Thou, O King Who art on the throne,
  Who didst make for me the day in its season;
I in the wilderness of the mountains,
  Thy warmth sheltered me from the cold.

It is Almighty God who takes the initiative. He has already done so. The Good Shepherd is ever looking for his lost sheep. He has died for each one of us, and is alive again. It is not the sheep who must search for the shepherd. Without him life is a wilderness; and often it is only when he is accepted that one can realize this. And when he is accepted the wilderness begins to blossom, the desert starts to live.

Many are the ways of evil habits
    To disturb the flesh of the sinful;
O Christ, ere I am laid in the tomb,
    Place Thou the power of Thy righteousness within me.

Evil habits grip us through our thoughts. Only someone with the power of Christ can cope with them. And we are given one life in which to let him do that.

Thou throned King of glory,
    Thou great Being Who hast redeemed me
From the foolish ways of sin
    To which my nature cleaves;

He can indeed cope with us—however bad we may have become. Nothing is beyond his almighty power to heal, however deeply attached—enslaved—we may be to this or that sinful way. Is anything more foolish than to refuse his offer to pardon, heal, enliven?

From sins corrupt
    Which have caused temptation to my soul,
From the sins deceiving
    That would conquer me despite my will.

Self—selfish ambition, self-centredness, self-esteem— develops into many sins. Like gangrene it will eventually kill the soul; for selfishness rots love. The deceiver, the devil, the 'father of lies', says 'be a getter— *get* all you can out of life.' Christ says 'be a giver—*give* all you can to the world around you.' The first is the way of death, the second the way of life. At last this is realized:

Though mine were the world
    And all the wealth upon its surface,
Though mine were every treasure,
    All pomp and all grandeur;

Though I should get and have them in my grasp,
    I would give them all away,

If but the Father of salvation
    Might with His arm encircle me.

Now there is a true sense of values.

O Thou great God enthroned,
    Succour me betimes with Thy goodness;
Make my sins unclean
    To part from me this night.

No one can do this on his own. The Christian Way provides
no 'do it yourself' kit. 'You can't pull yourself up to heaven
by your own shoelaces.' We can only let Christ take over.
Nothing less is needed than unconditional surrender to the
Lord of all.

For the sake of Thine anguish and Thy tears,
    For the sake of Thy pain and Thy passion,
Good Son of Mary, be in peace with me
    And succour me at my death!

He will indeed rescue all who ask him. Did he not die for each
one of us? Can we not hear him saying from the cross, 'do
you think I did all this for you, just to leave you alone?' Suc-
cour, help, rescue me—in my state of deathly existence.

Thou art my precious Lord,
    Thou art my strong pillar,
Thou art the sustenance of my breast:
    Oh part Thou from me never!

Everyone needs something to lean on for support. One's pride
may try to deny this. But bereavement, apparent or real
failure, acute fear, and other experiences can teach this.
Worldly consolations can be removed in a flash. In order to
face reality one needs some of such experiences.

For mine afflictions forsake me not,
    For my tears' sake do not leave me!
Jesu! Thou likeness of the sun,
    In the day of my need be near me!

'Man's extremity is God's opportunity.' We may have to get to the end of our tether—be humbled by suffering—before we are prepared to swallow our pride and hand our lives over to God. But this is the necessary prelude to joy, for he is 'the Light of the world'.[2]

> Thou great Lord of the sun,
>> In the day of my need be near me;
> Thou great Being of the universe,
>> Keep me in the surety of Thine arms!

His light is so strong that it dazzles, blinds us. 'The darkest place is at the foot of the lighthouse.' When we want him, and he seems nowhere around, he is especially close. Then we have to learn a new joy, that of faith—just trusting all the time that 'underneath are the everlasting arms'.[3] This is not 'blind faith', for the Bible, Christian experience, and real gratitude for all that he has done for us in our lives already, make this trust very reasonable indeed.

> Leave me not in dumbness,
>> Dead in the wilderness;
> Leave me not to my stumbling,
>> For my trust is in Thee, my Saviour!

When worldly consolations have been removed from us, at least for a time, we begin to learn to rely on spiritual consolations. In our misery or fear our thoughts turn to the invisible God. In this way sorrows are turned into rich blessings. After we have learnt something of this lesson, newly-found spiritual consolations may also disappear. For a person is being trained to love God with pure, unselfish love. For up till now there has been a certain natural, though unconscious, element of cupboard love in our attitude towards him. The serious follower of Christ may now find that his prayer, Communion, Bible reading, and so on, have 'gone dead' on him.

> Though I had no fire,
>> Thy warmth did not fail me;

95

> Though I had no clothing,
>   Thy love did not forsake me.

Even in this desolation there are joys. 'I'm getting nothing
out of my religion, Lord, so at last I'm really going to give
You a little bit of love—free.' But the extraordinary thing is
that he accepts me as I am—'just as I am'. And after having
some experience of being cut down to size in 'the night of
sense', a person begins to realize that he is nothing. And yet
Christ died for me! Incredible!

> Though I had no hearth,
>   The cold did not numb me;
> Though I knew not the ways,
>   Thy knowledge was around me.

So far human attempts to co-operate with God have been
based on reason. Now he takes his disciple a stage further in
learning utter dependence on him. Neither can human consolations be relied on, nor even spiritual experiences. By faith
and reason alone a person seems to have kept going. Now
there is no understanding any more. Nothing is 'reasonable'
now. It's just faith. Thank goodness God knows—under-
stands. We don't. It may take every ounce of courage to go
through with this.

> Though I was in weakness,
>   The hinds showed me kindness;
> Though I had no light,
>   The night was as the day.

Despite our lack of understanding, God turns out to be in
complete control. Reliance on him results in our needs being
met from unexpected sources.

> Though I had no bed,
>   I lacked not for sleep,
> For Christ's arm was my pillow,
>   His eye supreme was my protection.

Possessions can be stolen or destroyed. Human beings can be unreliable, or die. Christ alone is utterly dependable—and for ever. The only real security is Christ himself.

> Though I was forlorn,
>   Hunger came not near me,
> For Christ's Body was my food,
>   The Blood of Christ, it was my drink.

Christ gives us security. He nourishes us with himself—his love, his own perfect life-giving life. Awareness of him will now be beyond awareness. He is sensed (if that term can be used at all) at a level deeper than spiritual sensitivity. 'Blessed are those', said Jesus 'who have not seen and yet believe.'[4]

> Though I was without reason,
>   Thou forsookest me not a moment;
> Though I was without sense,
>   Thou didst not choose to leave me.

Like the first disciples Jesus' friends all down the ages have to 'put out into the deep'.[5] They are like swimmers, well out of their depth. They cannot touch bottom, nor hold on to the old well-loved rocks that had previously steadied them; nor even see the distant horizon. There is neither life-jacket nor life-belt. It can be terrifying. Alone. The awful feeling of being a lost soul who deserves to die. Why was I ever born? There can be a sense of losing one's reason, and therefore becoming out of control, and separated from all mankind by an unbridgeable gulf. But no: the Christian is simply learning that God is with him, in him, at a level deeper than the most sensitive spiritual intuition can detect. For it is not we who hold him, but he who is holding us.

> Though the stones were diamonds,
>   Though they were dollars of gold,
> Though the whole ocean were wine,
>   Offered to me of right;

97

> Though the earth were of cinnamon
>> And the lakes were of honey,
> Dearer were a vision of Christ
>> In peace, in love, in pity.

To reach this stage is to begin to live indeed! It means that this world's consolations can be enjoyed, if they don't divert from God. But there is no longer the urge to fight for them. Power, ambition, money—self-indulgence—such things take on a new and repulsive look. The desire for these has brought all the misery in human history. Now Christ has shown his total revolutionary way to peace and joy. And so we come to the climax of the poem. It is a great outburst of longing to live in ever closer intimacy with Christ.

> Jesu, meet Thou my soul!
>> Jesu, clothe me in Thy love!
> Jesu, shield Thou my spirit!
>> Jesu, stretch out to me Thine hand!

8 *A CHURCH AHEAD OF OUR TIME?*
Glimpses of an eighteenth-century phenomenon

Disestablished, nonconformist, and illegal. Such a description can now be applied increasingly to the Christian Church in one country after another. The pattern in fact follows that course.

First a Church is disestablished. In a modern pluralist society special patronage is less and less likely to be given to one body of people, however numerous they may be. Such is the case, for example, with Roman Catholics in the Irish Republic. In fact there are hardly any state or established Churches now left in the world, Scotland and England being among the very few remaining countries to preserve this status.

Next comes the nonconformist stage, when government policies lead to a head-on collision with Christians, as in some atheist states today. The abortion issue in fact, in our own National Health Service, in which a doctor's promotion may be jeopardized if he obeys a conscience at variance with permitted practice, may be a foretaste of trouble in Britain.

And finally, the Christian Church—and perhaps all religions—are made illegal, as in contemporary Albania.

It should therefore be quite obvious where we are heading. In fact it has all happened before. As the Bible tells us, 'there is nothing new under the sun.'[1] Circumstances have of course changed, and for that reason many people have not noticed the underlying trends. For, at first sight, there seems little comparison between sectarian feuds in the past, and united Christians facing an atheist or agnostic government in the future.

But look a bit closer at our country's experience. (And who will be so foolish as to ignore either his own personal or our common experience?) What we see in the past is a country in which everyone was nominally a church member, although only a minority of them might be serious followers of Christ. Almost all were influenced by economic, political, and social factors—and the nominal 'Christians' entirely so. When inevitable friction arose, even at times leading to civil war, religious motives were loudly proclaimed by anyone who thought they would serve his own—not infrequently selfish —purposes. But a really close look at Scotland's religious past reveals also a surprising degree of Christian co-operation that the reader of popular elementary textbooks would never suspect.[2]

Now every major denomination in Scotland since the Reformation has not only had its heyday, when it could boast the allegiance of almost everyone over large areas, but also it has had its time 'in the heather'. For two and a half centuries after the Middle Ages finally came to an end, hardly anyone could visualize a pluralist society with the option of belonging to a church of one's choice. As far as the government was concerned, the denomination that supported it would in turn be supported by it. In such circumstances rival churches with differing political affiliations could hardly be tolerated. Hence that disastrous jockeying for position that makes post-Reformation history painful reading.

We shall now have a close look at one of these churches while it was out 'in the heather'. The fact that it had been disestablished brings it at once into line with most churches today the world over. Naturally its disestablishment made it 'nonconformist'. We shall think of that status in relation to a hostile government and individuals, and not to the real or supposed animosity of another Christian church that had supplanted it. And we shall notice that this church, throughout the first half-century of its period of deepening trial became increasingly illegal. In fact state laws were designed to ensure its abolition. In this, however, they failed, though they came very near to success.

Which of the churches then are we to study? They all have much in common, not least fortitude and heroism. But one body of Christians was unique, for it alone could get no outside help. Roman Catholics, while persecuted, were able to turn to Ireland and the Continent. Presbyterians found support from English Puritans. The native Scots Episcopalians might have expected help from what was then the united (episcopal) Church of England and Ireland; but that body, being 'established' would, or could, have nothing to do with its Episcopalian sister in Scotland. The latter, when its turn came to be out in the heather had to go it alone. And in this respect it makes its story all the more contemporary. For modern governments can be—quite naturally—very jealous of foreign interference. And we shall see some very close parallels between the outlawed Scots Episcopalians of the eighteenth century and, for example, contemporary Chinese Christians and others who have much to teach us today.

Costly religion is real

'In all parts of the Highlands where I officiated the apparent devotion of the people was extremely remarkable, and very affecting ...'[3] So wrote Bishop Robert Forbes in his journal in 1770. And no wonder. 'These were dauntless shepherds and exemplary flocks' is an historian's comment, 'who loved their God so well that they were ready to stand for hours in the driving rain or the winter snow rather than lose the opportunity of joining in the prayers they had known since their childhood's days.'[4] If we are inclined to think that these people were quite different—though certainly hardier—from ourselves, we might just note a scene that was described long after there was freedom of religion in Britain, though still great poverty in the north. St Mary's—still today the only church of any kind in Glencoe—had not been built when a visitor described a scene that took place in 1872. 'There were about two hundred worshippers' he wrote, 'and, as I looked upon them, every knee bent on the grassy moss, and every head bowed low repeating the words of our venerable liturgy, I felt myself rebuked by the earnestness of their devotions. There they meet, Sunday after Sunday, in the summer

101

evenings, under the fir trees at the bridge over the Coe ...
When he preached the clergyman seemed thoroughly in
earnest [the writer had no Gaelic] and the attention with
which he was listened to was deep and profound.'[5] In the
previous century other writers had been very impressed by
their experiences of Episcopalian worship, Wesley among
them.

About another district in the Highlands comes this comment: 'How steadfast through all difficulties and dangers,
penal laws, proscribed worship, clergy hunted like partridges
in the mountains—still true were those thousand people in
Strathnairn and Moy.' And then follows the crux of the
matter: 'Religion then was a real thing, for it cost
something.'[6]

And in these days of widespread concern about money,
we might well take to heart another comment. 'The piety
and patient endurance of the poverty-stricken non-jurors will
convey to coming generations a lesson which the possession of
the richest endowments could never teach.'[7] For it is a re-
current theme in the history of the whole Christian Church
that material wealth goes hand in hand with spiritual
poverty. So instead of lamenting Britain's current inflation,
perhaps we should thank God that he is thereby turning our
attention largely away from those temporalities—some institutions, clergy status symbols, and a mass of other parapher-
nalia that can weigh down the Church and divert mankind's
attention from the simplicity of Christ.

Flock, not fold

But what would become of the laity if all these temporalities,
these possessions, this massive institutionalism, were removed? How could the people be nourished spiritually? Well
it is apparently happening in the Far East now. As one
Chinese Christian has stated, 'Christianity in China is becoming more and more simple. It consists of groups of Christians here and there gathered around Jesus Christ in word and
sacrament. It now uses very few church buildings.' And his

interviewer added, 'the Church as a whole does not have structures such as synods.'[8]

We shall now take a closer look at the laity. And first a visitor's impression of Linshart in Aberdeenshire, and one of the biggest Episcopalian congregations to have survived the troubled eighteenth century. In 1795 he wrote that the church could 'contain more than a thousand people', and added that 'the first thing that struck me was the strongly marked faces of the people, which betokened not only sense and sharpness, but also a serious frame of mind.'[9]

Having been ejected from the old Scots church buildings, and then having had their new 'meeting houses', in many cases, burnt after each successive Jacobite Rising, the poverty-stricken Episcopalians either had no churches at all, or else the plainest and simplest of buildings. And in other respects they anticipated not only the modern trend in simple, functional architecture, but also in liturgical practice. For example, they stood for the offertory, or laying the bread, wine, and alms on the altar. This was one symbolic expression of their belief that the Holy Communion is an offering of the whole congregation and not just that of the priest.

House church

The current house church movement, where Christians are finding an intimacy and fellowship that seems rarely to exist in ordinary church buildings, was of course common practice in the eighteenth century. In a house in Baron Taylor's Lane, Inverness, for example, the clergyman with his very small legal number of people for whom he was allowed at that time to conduct worship, would assemble on the ground floor; but a hole in the ceiling enabled a very much larger congregation of unspecified size to gather in the loft and take part with those below. And celebrating the Holy Eucharist on a kitchen table—out of sheer necessity—is nothing new either. Meanwhile prayer book services were in daily use at Castle Leod, for example, and in many other places. In less powerful households there might be a 'little concealed oratory, where

103

the family ... could keep their service books and say their prayers in times of trouble.'[10] This is reminiscent of those icon corners which are a feature of even the poorest Eastern Orthodox homes. Where such a place however could not be had with safety, prayer books might be buried in the garden, and dug up for use on Sundays.

But open-air sites for secret worship have always made the greatest appeal to Scots. And perhaps the most impressive of these 'sacred hollows' which were used by Episcopalians is that at Dunlichity in Strathnairn.[11] This conical depression can accommodate on its slopes hundreds if not thousands of worshippers, and the slightest sound within it carries from one side to the other. There are other sacred hollows, such as those at Ballachulish, which can easily be seen from the road.[12]

When a new church was opened at Keith at the end of the century, it was a humble thatched cottage. And in his sermon on this occasion Alexander Christie said, 'We have hitherto, like the Ark of God, been removed from place to place ... but his church was as venerable, whatever a giddy or grace-less world may think, "in an upper room", in "a hired house", in "a den or cave of the earth", as in "an ivory palace". These are but circumstantials, and nowise affect her existence, so ought never to discourage or puff up her members.'[13]

The laity—the 'people of God'

There is much debate today about the place of the clergy in the church. How much of their work can be done by laymen? In the early nineteenth century when churches, hitherto classed as illegal, were beginning to enjoy a new freedom, an Episcopal priest was sent—for the first time for some years—to Skye. And there, we are told, 'he found many families, and a number of individuals scattered here and there, who are sounder churchmen and better versed in our tenets than in many other places where they are blessed with the ministry of a clergyman. They allow no

Sunday to pass but they assemble in groups' for worship, and that many families use the morning and evening prayer book services daily. And with regard to Christian instruction our informant goes on, 'several of the young people also, from their earliest infancy, have been tutored ...'[14] A similar situation exists in Iceland today, where American Episcopalian servicemen, visited by a chaplain only monthly, hold weekly services, run a Sunday school, visit the sick, and provide each other with Christian fellowship.

In an age when every belief is questioned it is all the more vital that Christians should have a thorough grasp of their religion. And one quotation will serve to illustrate a too frequently overlooked aspect of this 'underground church' in its century of trial. Towards the end of the period we are told that 'the church was still cherished, her gifts prized, and amid the greatest difficulties numbers still remained true and faithful to the old religion of their forefathers, and that not from ignorant prejudice, but from well-grounded conviction.'[15] And Robert Forbes explained the basis of this belief when he wrote about the future profession of someone preparing for ordination. He wrote, 'what a knowledge ought he to have of the Scriptures, and of the Fathers, at least of the first three centuries? from whom we have not only the Scriptures delivered down to us, but also that pure, original, and catholic tradition, by which alone we are to explain them.'[16]

Children were taught the church catechism at home by their parents, and the clergy produced booklets to help them.

It took a well-instructed laity to defend their Church. The official principle in Scotland was that a lay patron, or patrons, should choose its own clergyman. So they did. Right across at least the northern half of Scotland, in parish after parish, they chose Episcopalians—and then were told that they couldn't have them, despite the fact that many of them, at first, were not anti-government Jacobites. It was rather like some atheist states today where freedom of religion is only official. The laity's defences of their position make interesting reading, tackling the situation not only from the legal angle but also from the doctrinal.

A typical letter, from the Black Isle, shows people objecting to the fact that the intrusion of a non-Episcopalian would result—in those days—in the discontinued use of the Lord's Prayer at public worship. The letter points out that all other Churches in Christendom use it; then why should they alone be debarred, when Christ himself taught us to pray it? And in the Cabrach, in Banffshire, the laity were so desperate that they wrote to Queen Anne herself explaining that they had invited a clergyman to fill their vacancy who had 'taken the oaths to your Majesty', but were then faced with official opposition. Their concern about this matter was on account of the fact, they wrote, 'that we cannot safely abandon our ancient Communion which we judge agreeable to the Word of God, and thus cut ourselves off from the whole Catholic Church under heaven, by incorporating with a society [i.e. the established church] we fear may be in a state of schism.' The lack of dogmatism here is noteworthy: they simply state 'we fear may be ...' And they continue, 'we judge it an insufferable usurpation to have the Westminster Confession foisted in at baptism in lieu of the Apostles' Creed, and so our children instead of being entered into the Christian religion, made proselytes to a faction.' The letter is very lengthy, and states that no one in their parish believed in the said 'large and bulky confession', which they consider to be full of 'the abstrusest and most thornie points' in theology.[17]

The Lord's Prayer is of course nowadays used by all Christians, and the Westminster Confession no longer forced upon any unwilling person. These old controversies are simply mentioned to illustrate the fact that the laity were concerned about biblical teaching. And Episcopalians described themselves both as 'catholic' and as 'protestant'. How successful they were in reconciling what, at least in Northern Ireland today, appear to some people as diametrically opposed standpoints, is a question that lies outwith the scope of this study.

What we must note however is that ordinary folk knew why they believed in this particular Christian tradition, and genuinely loved it—as our next 'glimpse' will show.

By mid-century the 'quality and gentry' of a north-east parish had apparently decided to appoint a clergyman who did subscribe to the 'bulky confession'. For doing so they received 'The humble address of the poor farmers and others' who stated, 'We always have been willing to submit to all your demands and commands in worldly matters ... You have changed our old farms. You have rais'd our old rents. You have taken possession of all our old money ...', and now 'our religion is we fear to be taken from us, for what reason we know not.' They add, 'It is all the comfort we have in life.' And the letter ends with the significant reminder 'that forc'd prayers are no devotion'.[18]

Trouble could come to such people from very unexpected quarters. For example the Lord Advocate entirely illegally— early in the century—ordered the closing of King's College Chapel, Aberdeen, because the principal used the prayer book there. And parishioners could go to their church on a Sunday only to find, to their surprise and horror, dragoons occupying it for the weekend, and playing cards therein. By the beginning of the century the people of at least the northern half of Scotland were quite used to the sight of troops or other armed officials protectively escorting the new minister—whom they had not 'called'—into their church. There had been fierce rioting, but apart from those who actively supported one or more of the Jacobite risings the policy of the Episcopalians during the eighteenth century was almost exclusively that of non-violence. And that was certainly the official standpoint of this church, even though the Earl of Mar was chiefly supported by its members, and its prayer book services only used for church parades during the '15' rising.

Quite the most well-known painting of this church during this period is Brownlow's 'Baptism from Stonehaven Gaol'. In Jacobite times three priests were put into the tolbooth, and the picture shows fisherfolk secretly holding up a baby in a creel to be baptized at the barred prison window. It was indeed a risky business for them, for baptism by an illegal clergyman was an offence; and not only the parent of a child at Keith, but the two witnesses and the householder were gaoled for this 'crime'. The officiant apparently died before the case was heard in court. Near the sacred hollow, already mentioned, in Strathnairn is a roughly hollowed boulder which was used as a font. Otherwise, as in the earliest days of Christianity, baptisms were performed wherever there was water. On one occasion snow was melted for the purpose—but of that story, more anon.

Christian initiation is being widely discussed today, and not least the relationship between baptism and confirmation. The appearance of a bishop to confirm anyone was a rare event in many districts in the later eighteenth century, and when Robert Forbes did his well-documented tours—not knowing when he or any other bishop might pass that way again—he would even confirm infants. This practice, as well as the use of chrism or anointing with oil, reflects the ancient practice, still used by the Eastern Orthodox Church, of regarding baptism and confirmation as one rite. Whether or not the western Churches will return to this practice remains to be seen.

Forbes's Journals include some vivid descriptions of Confirmation and Holy Communion services. Here is one that took place in Strathnairn on St Peter's Day, 1770:

At the chapel of Brin ... Began worship 'twix 11 and 12 to an audience of 7 or 800 people, young and old, and therefore a tent (the first time I ever performed worship in a tent, the people being on a rising ground over against my face, and forming a kind of semi-circle about the tent) was set up, as the chapel, a cross, would contain only about 500. Preached from Acts 8.14,15,16,17, Mr Allan [Cameron] resuming the discourse in Gaelic. Then we went into the chapel, where baptized ... to the number of 50, and confirmed 350, young and old, during which time the catechist, Andrew Mackintosh, was reading the Scriptures in Gaelic to the multitude about the tent. The greatest order and regularity was observed, gentlemen and farmers waiting on to direct those to be baptized and confirmed, to come in at one door and go out at another ... Left Brin 'twixt 5 and 6, leaving Mr Allan Cameron to finish all with prayers and exhortation in Gaelic, and, as one day would not suffice, to intimate worship to begin Sunday next 'twix 10 and 11, and that the Holy Eucharist was to be celebrated. Mounted Highland garrons once more ...[19]

Later he was back at Brin, and preached to over a thousand people.

The Lord's own service

Throughout the period there was a continual attempt to head this Church back towards the original primitive Christian practice of a weekly communion. As our own contemporaries would put it, 'The Lord's own service for the Lord's own people on the Lord's own day.' But after the common medieval practice of only communicating at Easter, and the extreme rarity of any Communion services in many districts after the Reformation—with intervals of years sometimes— it was an uphill struggle. But there was no notion of a free-for-all invitation. Holy Communion had to be approached with becoming penitence, humility, and a genuine desire to follow Christ. Communion tokens were issued to those who might communicate, but withheld from the impenitent until there was a sign of a change of heart and desire to amend, and they had received absolution. In the case of public scandals, which give the Church a bad name, a public penance might be required. And a service of preparation would generally precede a 'Communion Sunday', with a thanksgiving service on the Monday.

Before going to communion the communicants' 'self-preparations were long and searching', we are told, and 'they would be up and occupied in their devotions from a very early hour'.[20] Some would walk, fasting, fifteen miles to a service. And at Ballachulish there is one of the older chalices in use, dated 1723, from which local clansmen communicated before dying at Culloden. A very contemporary touch was their use of 'the Wee Bookies', as they were called. These were reprints of the text of the Scottish Liturgy (or Communion service) many of which were called for in the course of the eighteenth century. But the plainness of services was due not so much to principle as to necessity, and this is indicated by the attempts to beautify churches which had already begun as soon as penal laws began to be relaxed.

Not least on account of Christ's command 'do this in remembrance of me', some of the sacred elements (the consecrated bread and wine) at Holy Communion would be 'reserved' or set aside for those—such as the sick—who could not get to a service. This practice used to be described as 'the altar coming to' the people.[21] But in emergencies the next best thing had to be done; and it is said that John Maitland, 'chyrurgeon [i.e. surgeon] of the soul' attached to Ogilvie's regiment at Culloden, communicated the dying Lord Strathallan on that fatal battlefield using the only elements available—oatcake and whisky.[22] And after all, if Communion is the Christian soldier's battle-ration for life, the incident was not so extraordinary as it may seem.

Integrity

What were these people like? One's chief problem in trying to answer that question is that ordinary folk normally didn't get written up, and the records of public figures who were on the losing side might be falsified or destroyed.

One man who stands out in particular was Alexander, Lord Forbes of Pitsligo. He was not only deeply religious, but like not a few of his fellow-churchmen regarded the Jacobite risings as crusades. It was all very contemporary. In fact the relation between religion and politics is the chief topic today of heated arguments at meetings of the World

Council of Churches. And Lord Pitsligo was one of those who believed that Dutch William and his parliament in Scotland had put down the true Church. It had not been an act of a General Assembly. And if, for the moment, we overlook the fact that one lot of Christians was then replaced by another, we are face to face with the whole question of the use of force in achieving a desired end. That question no doubt looked somewhat different in the days before world wars, poison gas, and H-bombs.

Pitsligo was 67 when Charles Edward raised his standard at Glenfinnan. To the elderly Episcopalian the young prince was the rightful heir to the throne, and would remove the severe penal laws against his own beloved Church. A number of his neighbours joined him, and we are told that before setting off on horseback he lifted his hat and prayed, 'O Lord, thou knowest that our cause is just!' On the arrival of his party at the prince's camp an onlooker wrote later, 'It seemed as if religion, virtue, and justice, were entering the camp under the appearance of this venerable old man . . .'[23]

Suffering is the acid test of anyone's character, and Pitsligo's courage, humility and humour after the ' '45' justified his reputation. For he was a hunted outlaw, disguised as a beggar, and frequently living—and praying—in a cave. He was even once asked by soldiers to show them this cave, which he did, and watched their cautious approach with great amusement!

Another, but briefer glimpse of Christian behaviour, comes from a story about the MacDonalds of Glencoe. This clan was Episcopalian,[24] and during the risings naturally had memories of the notorious massacre which had been instigated against them largely by the Master of Stair. We are told that

> while Prince Charlie's army lay at Kirkliston, the prince, in his anxiety to save [a later] Lord Stair from molestation, proposed that the Glencoe men should be marched to a distance from his residence, lest memories of ancient wrongs might move them to deeds of vengeance. When this

proposal was made to the Glencoe men, their reply was that, if they were considered so dishonourable as to take revenge upon an innocent man they were not fit to remain with honourable men, nor to support an honourable cause. It was only by much persuasion that they were induced to overlook what they regarded as an insult, and prevented from taking their departure.[25]

The mysterious Appin murder, in which a notorious Campbell factor was shot, is a story almost as well known as the Massacre of Glencoe. The blame for it was falsely laid on James Stewart, or 'James of the Glen' (Duror)—a member of another Episcopalian clan—and he was unjustly condemned. A Cameron offered to bring fifty men and rescue him, but Stewart refused, alleging 'that such an attempt, would, no doubt, be attended with more hurt to his country than his life was worth.'[26] Before being hanged he professed his allegiance to his own Church, and prayed Psalm 35— which 'was afterwards known throughout the Western Highlands as *Salm Sheumais a' Ghlinne*—James of the Glen's psalm.'[27]

Talking of Camerons, they had the reputation in some quarters of being the bravest of the clans. They formed another stronghold of episcopacy, and were led by the justly famous 'Gentle Lochiel'. The latter's brother was the beloved 'Doctor Archie' who tended the sick and wounded among both friend and foe. His execution—and its circumstances— seven years after Culloden, did considerable harm to the government's already appalling reputation for injustice in the Highlands. Just before his death he wrote, 'I die a member (tho' unworthy) of that Church in whose communion I have always lived, the Episcopal Church of Scotland.'[28]

Of course there were obscure, though no less important, folk like John Macnaughton. He was either a footman or a watchmaker, and preferred to be hanged after the ''45' than to gain a reprieve and an income for life at the expense of betraying anyone. He was a member of an Edinburgh congregation, now Old St Paul's, of which we have rare and valuable records[29]—even of some services held in private houses. The office bearers, mid-century, appear to have been very ordinary citizens with a sprinkling of professional men like Sir Stuart Thriepland. This doctor accompanied Prince Charles while the latter was a hunted fugitive, and later became President of the Royal College of Physicians.

Another name that appears in lists of office bearers is that of Henry Raeburn, who may have been the great artist himself. Certainly a number of the most famous Raeburn portraits were of known members of this congregation, for many of the nobility had houses in Edinburgh or at least stayed there from time to time. One reads for example of a Seaforth and a MacDonald of Sleat baptism, and Eglinton and Gordon of Glenbucket weddings. (Readers may well be surprised over some of these, that they were conducted by Episcopalian clergymen.) By this time Episcopal clergy had been ejected, at long last, from almost all the old parish churches; the one at Kilmaveonaig, Blair Atholl, however, has remained in the same hands till the present day. Meanwhile not a few well-known public figures had their babies christened and their daughters married in the capital. As the older priests died one difficulty in replacing them lay in the fact that school and university teaching posts were debarred to avowed members of this Church at a period when part-time teaching enabled students to support themselves during their years of higher and ordination training. Swearing allegiance to the reigning monarch was not the stumbling-block so much as the enforced subscription to the Westminster Confession. If clergymen who existed during the second half of the century were often of exceptional calibre, they were relatively few in number. So, if you wanted their services you might well have had to seek them out. Which all goes to show, does it not, that those who deliberately foster a policy today of reducing the number of priests can go too far?

It is not surprising therefore to find Christians joining the only church which might be available to them, while really preferring membership of another. Nor is there always clear evidence now to show to which church a particular layman belonged. Flora MacDonald, the heroine, may be a case in point, during the first fifty-two years of her life. When she was a prisoner on board ship she told an inquirer that 'she had only a prayer book',[30] and evidence for Presbyterian dislike of such objects has been much popularized. Nor is she an isolated case. When that champion of Gaelic, Samuel Johnson, made his tour of the Western Isles in 1773 he not only is reputed to have said that 'the benevolence of the inhabitants ... cannot be enough praised,' but he also wrote, 'The gentlemen with whom I conversed are all inclined to [what he called] the English liturgy; but they are obliged to maintain the established minister ...'[31] (One of the gentlemen with whom he stayed was Flora MacDonald's husband.) This was no early example of 'anglicization'. A Perth clergyman wrote in 1743 that 'most of the clergy ... would sooner resign our several charges than give up the Scotch to use the English Communion Office, yea, the greatest number even of our laity would desert us should we attempt it.'[32]

The evidence seems to show that Scotland's spiritual heritage is far removed from that monochrome image which has been widely popularized. And even when at its lowest ebb, the Scottish Episcopal tradition, among others, was still revered; and early in the next century our most famous author, Sir Walter Scott, was to become at least an adherent.

Religion and culture

Cultural differences between Christians are a factor that we are having to face increasingly as the world shrinks. In the jet age we live in a global village, and not surprisingly many races are fearing the loss of their identity, and this is leading to a rising tide of nationalism. This trend is of great value to Christians, because it forces us to relate to each other at a much deeper, spiritual level. No longer can we delude ourselves that we have Christian fellowship when all our local church may be, in reality, is a collection of people united by a common racial or social culture pattern with Christianity as a kind of superficial top-dressing. Established churches are always in danger of trying to prop up their status by loudly proclaiming national superiority. A disestablished church may try to make its appeal largely to this or that stratum in society. Perhaps only in international religious communities, and especially the Little Brothers of Jesus, has this issue been faced realistically.[33]

Now an impartial observer—Professor Daiches—writes that in eighteenth-century Scotland 'outside the established church there were religious traditions that claimed to be more thoroughly national and more adequately linked with Scotland's past.' He mentions 'the greater human warmth and the greater links with tradition found in the Episcopalian way' of those days, and says that 'it was a strongly Scottish one' and that it was in their 'households that the older tradition of music and poetry were more likely to be preserved, especially in the north-east.' 'In the north generally', he adds, 'Episcopalians and Catholics kept up Gaelic . . . and bore no blame for the destruction of abbeys and churches and the suppressing of popular literature and festivities.'[34]

Despite the Protestant reformers' intention of giving people the Scriptures in a language they could understand, the hostility of some southern Lowlanders towards Highland culture left the Gael destitute of a Bible in his own language. And in those days the population of Scotland was far more evenly distributed than it is now, with a very large proportion of Gaelic speakers. Various attempts were made to rectify the omission, not least by two Episcopalian clergymen in particular, Robert Kirk and James Kirkwood. And Daiches' statement, quoted above, is born out by a verse in Kirk's edition of Gaelic metrical psalms:

Go leaflet boldly forth
With God's pure songs arouse them yonder;
Hail the generous land of Fionn,
The rough bounds and isles of the stranger.'[35]

The allusion to Fionn, the legendary 'King Arthur' of pre-Christian times among the Gael, would have horrified those with a puritanical turn of mind.

With regard to traditional Gaelic prayers, Alexander Carmichael's vast collection was made in the West Highlands and Islands, and at least one exceptionally beautiful prayer was noted down in Glencoe. It includes this verse which he translated:

Heavenly light directs my feet,
The music of the skies gives peace to my soul,
Alone I am under the wing of the rock,
Angels of God calling me home.[36]

In Linshart in Buchan, John Skinner senior had daughters who pestered him to write them poems. And no wonder! But his pastoral duties prevented him from exercising his talent to the full for composing often humorous Scots poetry. Of Skinner's most famous piece Burns wrote: 'the best Scotch song ever Scotland saw—"Tullochgorum's my delight!"'[37] And in a light-hearted way Skinner could convey serious lessons, as in 'Lizzie Liberty' in which he points out that liberty cannot be won except in the spirit of liberty. It is all very contemporary these days when countries are invaded in order, it is loudly proclaimed, that they may be 'liberated'.

There is of course also the political independence that may be sought from within a country itself. Scottish nationalism is an important issue today. If such a movement is exclusively an expression of love for one's own people, and for their welfare, then it can make an honest appeal to Christians. If, as is sometimes the case, nationalism fosters hatred of another race, it is decidedly un-Christian. And in a little incident among Episcopalian slate quarrymen of old we catch a glimpse of genuine Christianity at a time when there was much mutual dislike, and even hatred, between Scots and English. We are told that 'the men were not clear about certain workings of the quarry', so Stewart of Ballachulish 'got some Englishmen in to help. They all left but one man who married a MacDonald. When she died and he was too old to look after himself, his fellow quarrymen looked after him, he stayed one week at one house then moved on to the next home and so on till the end of his life.'[38]

If religion and politics were very much intertwined in eighteenth-century Scotland, then cultural and economic issues were to take their place in the following one. How this small, emerging former underground Church tried to cope with that situation lies outwith the scope of this study. But that does not mean that it is irrelevant today: far from it. In China, for example, the Christians are having to live down a western culture-pattern, and they aim 'to make the Church in China Chinese . . . national but not nationalistic'.[8] Sundar Singh gave Indians a vision of Christ as an Indian, and paved the way—surely more than anyone else—for a united Church in that sub-continent. Somehow all of us have to meet each other at a level deeper than culture; yet, being human, we express ourselves in a way that is natural to our own racial ethos. The most dangerous Christians in this encounter are those who are utterly unaware of the cultural element in their religion. If this were more widely recognized we should have better relations throughout Britain between Anglicans and Presbyterians. And no one surely can be more vividly and painfully aware of this than a native Scots Episcopalian.

Shortage of clergy

We hear a lot about the shortage of clergymen these days, or perhaps rather about the need to reduce numbers on account of the rising cost of living. Hence the training of non-stipendiary priests and full-time deacons, and of course discussions on the role of the laity. And it has happened before. We have seen something of the Episcopalian laity in the eighteenth century, and now we shall try to catch glimpses of the clergy. And to do this the more effectively we shall include the first half of the nineteenth century, for in many districts the poverty of the people and the shortage of priests left the latter with problems very similar to those of their predecessors of Jacobite times. Yes, and similar no doubt also to our own future.

John Murdoch taught in school, at Keith, from 7 a.m. to 4 p.m. (Tell that to your children!) He also indulged in manual work, presumably on his croft, just as Greek Orthodox priests do today. William Longmore, living earlier, had a tougher time of it. 'He was well known from Banffshire to Caithness' we are told, because when he was 'driven from one district by penal enactments, it was not long before he made his appearance in another, and large numbers of people, even in defiance of the law, not unfrequently flocked to his ministrations.'[39] Sunday School in such circumstances was exciting, and in Fochabers in 1746 'in the dark Sunday evenings the young people used to gather at Mr Mitchell's house, a thatched cottage, to be catechized.'[40] It was however much more common for the clergy to go to their people, and in view of the current price of petrol one hopes no one will have to try to emulate Alexander MacDonald, who successfully ministered to the people of Ardnamurchan for many years, walking between fifty and sixty miles every Sunday (there and back) to conduct a service! At least he had a contact with his people that a motoring clergyman misses, for they would join him *en route*.

Those were days when vitriolic abuse was all too common. Attempts to dislodge a clergyman were often made on the pretext that he was ignorant. Such men frequently turn out to have been university graduates. When accusations of Jacobitism failed, trumped-up charges of immorality might occur, as over John Williamson's supposed affair with a domestic servant at Redcastle. It came to nothing, but the authorities concerned left no stone unturned in their attack on a priest whose successful ministry ranged from the Black Isle to Lewis.

John Taylor was not so lucky. Though not a Jacobite he was paraded in the streets of Kirkwall and imprisoned in the unventilated hold of a ship. Some of his fellow-prisoners died, but he survived by sucking air in through the chinks of a door at night. He was then falsely accused of assisting someone to escape, and put in among diseased prisoners. Had it not been for the attention of one of his fellows, who was a doctor, he would have died. There are plenty of reports today of diabolical prison conditions, from many countries.

There is an extraordinarily generous presbytery report about Aeneas Morison who operated illegally in Strathpeffer. It says of his pastoral work that he baptized and absolved to such an extent that 'we have got few or no scandalous persons, especially in our vacancies, to submit to discipline.'[41]

Some of the clergy were of course staunch Jacobites, just as some today are keen members of a political party. John McLauchlan was very popular in north Argyll and kept Appin Kirk in his own care till as late as the ''45'. He 'acted as chaplain to the prince' we are told, 'and had a commission to be chaplain-general to the loyal clans'[42], i.e. Jacobites. After Culloden he had to make himself scarce.

The ultimate test

One of his colleagues however not only didn't get away after that disastrous affair, but was executed. Should we describe him as a martyr? For a cause, perhaps. But a *Christian* martyr? In the seventeenth century quite a number of people were executed in Scotland on account—as they believed—of their religion. But those who ordered the executions regarded their prisoners as being politically dangerous, and often with good cause. If this fact were more widely grasped we should have less sectarian animosity in Scotland today. And it is for this reason that Episcopalians are content simply to regard Robert Lyon as a very brave, and very young man from Perth, who had the courage of his convictions and—though only a non-combatant chaplain—had to die for them. Captured Roman Catholic priests, however, who had gone into battle sword in hand, were mercifully reprieved. Their executions, it has been suggested, might have caused international repercussions. But an Episcopalian, like Lyon, was defenceless.

His last letter was written from Carlisle castle a few days before his death on 28 October 1746. Here are some extracts from it:

My dear mother and my loving sisters,

... everything that could be looked on as comfortable in this world being denied me ... But blessed be my merciful God, they could not stop the inward consolations of God's Holy Spirit ... The miseries I have already undergone, and humanly speaking, am still to suffer, are undoubtedly inflicted upon me as a just reward and punishment for my manifold sins and iniquities ... to wean my heart from all inordinate affections to the follies and vanities of the world, to enlarge my heart with desires of being with Jesus, my Saviour ...

Grieve not for me, my dearest friends, since I suffer in a righteous and honourable cause, but rather rejoice that God has assisted me by his grace, the most unworthy of his servants, to act agreeably to my conscience and duty ... But since that God hath thought fit to warn me of my own mortality by giving me a summons to die a violent and barbarous death by the hand of man, I thank God for it ...

Pray then consider:

That God is perfect love and goodness; that we are not only his creatures, but his children, and as dear to him as to ourselves; ... and that all evils of afflictions which befall us, are intended for the cure and prevention of greater evils, of sin and punishment. And therefore we ought not only to submit to them with patience as being deserved by us, but to receive them with thankfulness as being designed by him to do us that good and to bring us to that sense of him and ourselves which perhaps nothing else would have done ...

... this separation will be but a very little while, and that though I shall leave you in a very wicked world, yet you are all under the care of a good God who can be more and better to you than I and all other relations whatever ...

He asks his mother to regard as her daughter the young woman Robert Lyon was to have married, and to remain faithful to that Church in which, he writes, 'I have the honour to die a very unworthy priest.' And he adds, 'the disciple is not to expect better treatment than his Lord and Master.'

Towards the end of this long letter he says, 'let us fervently pray for one another that we may have a joyful and happy meeting in another world ...'

We are told that 'upon the scaffold' he had 'the same calmness and composure of mind and the same decency of behaviour, as if he had been only a witness of the fatal scene.'[43]

Quality, not quantity

If we haven't got to that state mercifully in modern Britain, there is another kind of test which can be more severe than many people realize. At one stage Allan Cameron, a farmer's son, was the only clergyman of this reduced Church in the whole of Ross-shire; and despite his poor health he also served Appin, and was described as 'a missionary of the true apostolic order'.[44] To cope with that loneliness, responsibility and apparently hopeless outlook, he must indeed have lived close to Christ.

There are of course happier glimpses of this Church. We can see, for example, Paul MacColl standing at the top of the steps at Laroch stables, Ballachulish, preaching powerful and eloquent extempore sermons in both Gaelic and English to hundreds of open-air worshippers.[45]

But our fullest picture can be pieced together from glimpses of the rugged-looking Duncan Mackenzie or, as he was known far and wide, Parson Duncan. His base was upper Strathnairn, still well populated during his ministry from 1817 till his death in 1858. His people were numerous but exceedingly poor, and that poverty he shared, living on less than his stipend of £40 a year—one account says £15!—for his generosity could not be entirely hidden.

His parents had a smallholding at North Ballachulish, and we are told that Duncan was

> self-educated, and supporting himself from boyhood by the labour of his own hands, he earnestly sought opportunity of devoting himself to the ministry ... For it he sacrificed talents which would have led to distinction in any other profession. And nothing daunted by the extreme poverty of his church ...

he set about preparing for ordination. This included going to Aberdeen University, and there 'he became closely associated with his relative, Mr Ewen Maclauchlan the most eminent Gaelic scholar of his day.'[46] From then on he was to spend

> upwards of forty years in works of Christian philanthropy —acting in the most unostentatious and unsectarian manner, not only the part of the Christian minister, but also the medical adviser and trusty counsellor of the whole glen. The congregation, with the exception of three or four families, consists of the poor and working classes ...[47]

Soon his fame spread. We are told that 'people came from all parts of the Highlands, from Iona and John o'Groats House, to consult him as to their health', and that 'a particular friend, a chemist in Inverness, was empowered when he saw a certain mark on the ... prescriptions not to charge for them. So frequent were these *gratis* orders, that the benevolent druggist at last insisted on bearing half the sum so discounted to the poor patients.' Goodness as well as evil can be contagious. And we are told that 'some of his cures were very remarkable, and many ... were persuaded that' Parson Duncan 'not only prayed for those who consulted him, but also that he had a special gift of healing.'[48]

'But to the duties of his clerical office he mainly devoted himself.' And here is an account of a characteristic incident:

On one occasion ... a messenger was sent to him that a man and his wife would be at his chapel on a certain hour to have their baby baptized by him. A heavy snow storm came on that day, and after waiting in church for some time, Mr Mackenzie became anxious about the safety of the parties, and lest the young mother and her child might suffer from exposure to the cold. He accordingly set out on foot to meet them, got across the hill, and prevented them from coming on by baptizing the child in the open air, using a little snow which he placed in his own hand and melted ...

He was said 'to have been never at home',[49] and on foot, or on his white pony, ranged up Stratherrick or over to Dingwall. Once he turned up in Inverness 'having toiled all the forenoon through wreaths of snow, and walked on up to the knees in snow after his horse had given up and been left at a cottage on the way!'

He 'published in Gaelic an entirely new revision of the Book of Common Prayer, which, for beauty, precision, and power of expression, is not surpassed by any work in the language, and is the admiration of every Celtic scholar, as it has in fact become the book of private devotion of many of the peasantry of the Highlands, as well Presbyterian as Episcopalian.'[50]

We are told that 'in his labour of love he was assisted by his wife [Flora] and they denied themselves many necessaries for the sake of others.'[51] And today you can still see his spurs, which are kept as a sacred memento in St Paul's Church, Strathnairn.

Despite keen and responsible layfolk, how did this Church survive at all with so few priests? The answer is simple—catechists. One only wishes that we could discover more about these men—people like Alexander Mackay at Arpafeelie on the Black Isle—who held congregations together in many parts of the Highlands. On Sundays they would lead the prayer book service, and were licensed to translate into

Gaelic some authorized books of sermons; and in case of necessity could baptize. We are told that

> so much were they esteemed among the people—so strong and uncompromising was the people's attachment to the worship and ordinances of the Church—that in the absence of a clergyman the 'meeting house' was as largely attended, and the appointed services as reverently and devoutly conducted, as when he was present.

Their duties consisted 'also in catechizing the young and old in private houses',[52] and lists of those catechized include members of all social classes, not excluding the titled.

During the eighteenth and, to some extent also the early nineteenth, century the prospects of the clergy were clear: not 'advancement' but following the cross-bearing Christ in poverty, obscurity, hardship, and persecution. After the probationary period of being a deacon nothing other than simple priesthood could be expected—except of course becoming a bishop, which could have had no attractions whatever. (It was usual in those days—as it is once again become common practice now—not to address these men as 'my lord'). As there were no cathedrals there were neither provosts nor canons; and a dean was simply the priest appointed to 'hold the fort' during a diocesan vacancy, and preside over the election of a new bishop. He used no title. The threefold ministry of bishop, presbyter or priest, and deacon, which this Church believed in, was thus clearly demonstrated without confusion. There was no counterpart to the medieval titles which seemed to give the Church as well as the state a feudal structure. If ordained, after the deacon's year you were either a pastor or pastor of pastors. In either event you were evaluated not by worldly status symbols, but by the degree to which people believed you reflected Christ. And, with very few exceptions, it appears that the bishops and other clergymen of this Church during the hard eighteenth century—especially latterly—were of a high order. No doubt this had a potent influence on encouraging men, like John

124

Skinner senior, to leave security behind, join this Church, and offer himself for ordination. And in his case, for example, it is absolutely clear that politics could have played no part in his decision, for he was no Jacobite. And in fact, though not becoming a bishop, he gradually came to exercise a greater influence over this Church than anyone else during the time of his ministry, for spiritual leadership and ecclesiastical rank are two distinct phenomena in the Church—which may or may not coincide.

Apostolic bishops

James Gadderar's seal was a burning heart, the IHS monogram (representing 'Jesus') pierced by a cross, and the motto 'Amor meus crucifixus'—'my Love is crucified'.[53] Aberdeen, from the pre-Reformation Elphinstone to the present century, has had several outstanding bishops, and Gadderar must surely rank as one of these. His seal could have been used appropriately by not a few of his colleagues during the eighteenth century.

They were impressive men. Of Arthur Petrie of Moray, it was said that 'poor himself, living in a mere cottage, he made no pretence. He needed no outward grandeur.'[54] And

> tradition still relates the gratification with which Bishop Petrie ... was hailed when seen coming slowly up the glen on his little pony, his check plaid serving for gown and lawn sleeves ... So much respected did he become ... that the inhabitants of the districts he traversed, without distinction of creed, often strove who should get him as their guest.[55]

No wonder. We are told that if all 'went well' with the Church, 'he rejoiced in the midst of pain and bodily weakness', and that 'the pleasures of the body he had so entirely got above, that such a thorough conquest of them has been rarely seen in later times.'[56] Genuine holiness often evokes hostility, but there is nothing like it for breaking down barriers between otherwise good-hearted folk.

In those days a bishop remained in charge of a congregation, and without increase of stipend had to visit his diocese to confirm, act as a pastor of the clergy, and often train an ordinand in the humble cottage in which he himself lived. Travel expenses might be at least partly defrayed by special collections.

As a result we find that several of the eighteenth-century bishops resided in the north-east where there were relatively large congregations. And Petrie's successor but one, for the Moray diocese east of Inverness, was Alexander Jolly. This remarkable man was almost a hermit, living in two small upstairs rooms in Fraserburgh. His portraits show an alive, kindly, and ascetic face, and it appears that he rose daily for prayer at about 4 a.m.—except when he spent the whole night on his knees. The morning would be given to prayer and study, and his advice was not only sought far and wide but carried weight second to none in the Episcopal Church. At lunch-time someone would bring him a pot of something to eat; and in the afternoon he would go visiting—with children trotting alongside awaiting those ha'pennies and sweets he kept for them in his overcoat pockets. He used to send money to his clergy for their families, and visit them, but rarely held a synod, and never gave a 'bishop's charge' or sermon to his clergy. (He would no doubt have approved of that World War II slogan, 'Is your journey really necessary?')

From his upstairs room, surrounded by his well-known library, he exercised a strong, stabilizing, and unifying influence on his Church as it faced the trials of emerging after a century of persecution. Perhaps he was, latterly, too conservative. But of his faith there can be no doubt. He wrote:

Our strength (verily) is to sit still in quietness and in confidence; each in humble dependence studying and labouring at his post, to do all the good he can; and so the whole shall prove good and happy ... The times are cloudy and threaten storm; but when we look up, we know that the sun shines above the cloud, and will in due time dispel it.[57]

One senses a great depth of faith in some of these eighteenth- and early nineteenth-century bishops. They trusted God, and so were able to engender the strength of quietness and confidence among their people during troubled times. 'Let the world rub on as it pleases' wrote Robert Forbes of Ross,

> and craft and dissimulation prevail in a variety of shapes, our province is to be instant in season and out of season, etc [quoting St Paul] ... without being dazzled by the rich or awed by the great. If we lay the truth before folks, with all Christian prudence, and yet they will shut their eyes, let them answer for it to God and their own consciences ... In fine, if we do our parts conscientiously and wisely, let us leave the event to God, who will certainly do his part ...[58]

At any one time during the period we have been studying there were few bishops in this Church. But among them were men who, spending most of their time in one small place, earned the right to be called leaders, and were recognized as such both in their own dioceses and well beyond their bounds. And all this without the use of modern transport, telephones, and mass media communication. For real Christian leadership needs no aids.

Making American history

The image of the Church being 'run' by a kind of episcopal junta, directing affairs from frequent secret conclaves, could hardly have been further from the truth. In fact the bishops very rarely met at all. But when it was necessary, they could be swift to act.

It so happened that away across the Atlantic a new nation was born, and one of the dioceses, naturally wanting a bishop of its own, elected Samuel Seabury and sent him off to be consecrated in England. But this was most embarrassing for the English bishops, for they belonged to a state Church whose form of consecrating a bishop necessitated his swearing allegiance to the British crown.

It was then (or had already been) suggested that Seabury might try the Scots. So off he went, in 1784, to Aberdeen; and in no time the northern bishops gathered round him in secret and gave the Americans a bishop of their own. And that's why they call their Church 'Episcopal' rather than 'Anglican'. In fact the Society for the Propagation of the Gospel had already employed not a few Scots Episcopalians in what had previously been the American colonies, among whom James Blair had been given a supervisory position.

Christian unity

We have so far tried to see this Church simply as a body of Christians facing a hostile government and individual enemies. It is in this role that it has most to teach us today. But we have not yet reached the stage of realizing a united Christian front, and some inter-denominational glimpses from the eighteenth century may be instructive.

John Skinner's church was burnt by soldiers and his house pillaged. Fearing that he might lose some of his congregation to the parish church—for they had suffered a good deal already—he wrote a tract entitled *A Preservative against Presbytery*. Later, after the parish minister, a certain Mr Brown, had died, Skinner was asked where he himself would like to be buried. 'Lay me down beside Mr Brown' came the reply—'he and I got on very well together during life.'[59] No doubt neither would compromise, and so in traditional Scots fashion were able to respect each other and 'get on very well'. And the basis of this respect was something that is too often overlooked even today. On another occasion Skinner was

> passing a small dissenting place of worship at the time when the congregation were engaged in singing: on passing

the door ... he reverently took off his hat. His companion said to him, 'What! do you feel so much sympathy with this Anti Burgher congregation?' 'No,' said Mr Skinner, 'but I respect and love any of my fellow-Christians who are engaged in singing to the glory of the Lord Jesus Christ.'[60]

Although what is now called the 'ecumenical movement' was still two centuries away, our contemporary sharing of churches was already anticipated in the early eighteenth century. Apparently at both Dunfermline and Haddington there was an Episcopalian and a Presbyterian on the staff of the parish church. On Sunday mornings the former conducted the service according to the rites of his Church, and in the afternoon the latter did the same.

Christians who do it know that they grow together by praying together. Attempts at easier 'church-political' short-cuts to unity can have disastrous results. One would not suggest for a moment that Skinner's tract should be re-printed. But the relationship between him and the parish minister, in times of bitterness far exceeding anything we have experienced in twentieth-century Scotland, has surely something to teach us. There is of course a very great deal of friendly co-operation going on today. And it is increasing. But there is also still an apparent reticence in some quarters, not so much perhaps as the result of unfriendliness as of doubt. When William Hay was Bishop of Moray he was asked how one should deal with Christians whose beliefs one considered to be false. He simply replied, 'Excel them in life and doctrine.'[61] And if the word 'doctrine' sounds argumentative, we may simply add what his successor, that respected theologian Alexander Jolly wrote. After stating 'I continually pray for the healing of schism', he referred to Church principles, saying that 'it is surely the safest way to keep firm hold of them and maintain them in the primitive spirit of meekness, humility, and charity ...'[62]

The heart of the matter

By the beginning of the eighteenth century there were not a few keen Christians who were utterly sickened by Church controversy, which during the previous century had been exceedingly bitter, chiefly in southern Scotland. There seemed to them to be no connection between this bitterness and the cultivating of a relationship with Christ in one's heart. All those who have felt the desire for a deeper and authentic personal religion—which is a notable feature among younger adults today—will feel a kinship with these Christians.

George Garden, who had inherited the spirit of Leighton, and of the 'Aberdeen Doctors'—or divines—such as Henry Scougal, became the natural leader of like-minded men, especially among the laity in Aberdeenshire. His letters on contemplative prayer are steeped in scriptural language and quotations, and in references to internationally famous spiritual classics from all ages. Charges of a particular heresy were levelled against him by men of different denominations, but his published letters are his vindication. In them he emerges as a man of great sensitivity, Christian charity, and wisdom. And there is one tantalizing entry in a hostile report of 1710, that 'Dr Garden ... keeps up a settled society of unmarried men and women living together into the house of Rosehearty ...'[63] It sounds akin to the dual monasteries, of both monks and nuns, in Celtic times. And in these days of experimentation in new forms of monastic life, one cannot help wondering if this community at Rosehearty anticipated one of the current trends. But an 'underground church' doesn't usually keep records, so very unfortunately we know no more.

The Episcopal Church has undergone many changes since its century in the heather. And the one thing about it in those days that will surely make a wide appeal to many readers was its simplicity. The very height of praise was reached by anyone or anything if it were described as 'primitive and apostolic'. We have seen how they tried to live up to that standard—or should one say 'down'? For in adversity more and more of them came to value the Christ who 'humbled himself', and to learn painfully, with St Paul, that 'when I am weak then I am strong'.[64] The later medieval and Renaissance concept of a triumphalist Church was completely rejected during the course of the eighteenth century. It was in the nineteenth that it reappeared, and someone—very obviously not reared in the native tradition—even went so far as to build himself a 'bishop's palace' (now mercifully sold). And though we may well value an occasional special service in a large, packed church—which can be inspiring sometimes—it is interesting and significant that the saintly Bishop Jolly has not even a plaque to his memory in the Victorian cathedral of his former diocese. As someone put it—'a memorial to Jolly in a cathedral? He would turn in his grave at the very idea!'

Perhaps that humble man knew a prayer that was used by Alexander Monro, formerly principal of Edinburgh University who, like most Scottish university staff members had been ejected for his beliefs when William of Orange's reign began. He would certainly have approved of it. Here are some better known phrases from it—ones in fact that have appeared and re-appeared in prayer book revisions since the seventeenth century:

> O God, our present help in time of trouble ... grant that the Catholic Church may be so guided and governed by thy good Spirit that all who profess and call themselves Christians may be led into the way of truth, and hold the faith in unity of spirit, in the bond of peace, and in righteousness of life.[65]

The eighteenth, and even the early nineteenth century, is now well in the past. So many changes have taken place that one may well wonder what the Episcopalians of those days would think of their successors today. About that we can only speculate. What we can surely say truly is that this particular

131

'phenomenon' which we have been considering is now part of Scotland's common Christian heritage. To some of us it is one of the brighter glories in our rich and varied Scottish tradition. And as we look to the future, it encourages us to know how very many of the difficulties which we are now facing, and the possible trials that we may have yet to experience, have already been faced courageously—and often wisely—by our forefathers. And if they trusted in God, then surely so can we.

9 UNITY THROUGH SILENT PRAYER
A modern experience

'The week of *prayer for* Church unity' they call it. But very early on it had degenerated into 'the week of *preaching about* Church unity'. Annually someone in unfamiliar garments— a 'visiting artiste' as some sailors used to say—would step into your pulpit and preach a good, bad, or indifferent sermon. And for another year one could say 'here endeth' our local ecumenical adventure.

Of course in many parishes now the situation is very different and greatly improved. But there are still many where little if any advance has been made. And once development has got stuck, enthusiasm wanes and despondency is liable to set in. The movement towards Church unity, as many say, has lost momentum. And the reason, may I suggest, is that we have been inundated with far too much preaching at the expense of far too little praying.

Now some years ago three of us decided that something had to be done. We were respectively in charge of a Church of Scotland congregation, a Roman Catholic one, and an Episcopalian. Our churches were not so very much more apart from each other than a stone's throw or two, and we were in the midst of a fast-growing housing scheme on Edinburgh's outskirts. Our congregations were keen—keen as you get them when they know they are comparatively small minorities in a largely non-churchgoing world. The names of the Almighty were only known to most of our neighbouring children as swear-words. And youngsters abounded. They were typical of the vast mass of Britain's future adults.

Presenting a common front

In the face of such a situation—and it is becoming increasingly common—we Christians simply had to present a common front. The question was, How? In a major age of change, when everything is being questioned, and theologians are disinclined to agree, parish clergymen can be in a dilemma. It was not that we were particular sticklers for this or that doctrine. We had our hands full with pastoral affairs. But we also knew that we belonged to Christ's Church and not our own. It was his opinions that counted. His was the truth—not ours to play with.

'Man's extremity is God's opportunity', as the old saying goes. And my only reason for telling you what we did is to encourage those—who may still be nervous of starting—how very simply one can get going. The following account is a purely personal view of one of those who was involved at the start.

The three of us mentioned above decided simply to spread the matter out before the Lord. In penitence for our divisions, and in dependence on the Holy Spirit, we would together wait on God *in silence*. We split the difference between the larger churches and met first in the theologically 'middle' one—the Episcopal—which was also the smallest.

What about precedence? Could Roman Catholics receive a blessing from a clergyman who, to them, was not considered to be in holy orders at all? These, and many other objections, could cross one's mind. If one thought about such things for long enough, one would of course do nothing at all. Silence and simplicity provided the answer.

Members of all these congregations were invited to gather for prayer on a week-night. The clergymen involved, wearing ordinary everyday clothes, knelt side by side in a front pew. As it was my own church I welcomed the people and told them to pray in whatever posture they were used to. One of my colleagues read a short passage from the Bible. After half an hour's silence we said the Lord's Prayer, having decided

134

to use the form as practised in whatever church we met. A good congregation turned up, and tea followed in the hall.

Basic principles

We decided to repeat the experience, and also form a council committee. An informal 'ministers' fraternal' also met; and naturally the prospect of furthering joint activities was discussed at our respective congregational committees. Out of all this several principles emerged:

1 There must be no proselytizing. Now this may be so obvious that it sounds trite to mention it. Unfortunately, after experience in different parts of Scotland, I have deliberately placed it first.

2 We would not gaze at each other, thus focusing our attention on our differences, but would stand shoulder-to-shoulder facing the largely unbelieving world around us.

3 With national inter-church committees naturally concentrating on denominational differences—and thus via some newspapers whipping up old animosities—our need was to make friends with each other and take note of our similarities. Only in such an atmosphere could anything worth while develop and, eventually, if necessary controversial issues could be discussed amicably.

4 All controversial issues, meantime, were to be avoided like the plague.

5 Our three churches were to move together with no attempts at closer fellowship between any two of them. This would mean marching at the rate of the slowest, but it resulted in every one moving together. No individual, to my knowledge, was left behind.

And we did move. The silent half-hour meetings became regular practice, taking place in each of our church buildings in turn. And I remember after the second or third one, as we went into the hall, a layman and I both discovered that we had quite naturally found ourselves not praying that night

135

for each church in turn, but for the local Christians as *one body*.

Facing outwards

Parties and dances were held in the Church of Scotland hall —it being the biggest—and although cultivating friendship was our chief object, money made from tickets was used for our annual agreed Christian Aid project. For the latter we fixed on some object we could all work for together, like well-digging in India or a leper colony in Africa. And apart from the annual film-and-exhibition evening there would be a sponsored walk and various other activities.

A house-to-house visitation was organized locally, and every visitor had to go with a partner not of his or her own denomination. The visitors were given leaflets headed 'The local churches welcome you', and were instructed how to introduce themselves at each door. Names of those wishing to make contact with any of our churches were passed back to the minister or priest concerned. Whether or not any of us discovered new members, the chief result of this visitation was an invaluable strengthening of local Christian fellowship; and it also led to at least one deep, Christian friendship.

A combined carol service was held annually at the community centre—being 'neutral ground' as it were—and everyone invited. We also put up a notice board in one of our shopping areas, headed 'The local churches welcome you', and below that, in a row, the names of our churches in alphabetical order, with the telephone numbers of the clergy.

In a district of about 15,000 people in one square mile, with only city councillors to represent them who had other districts to attend to as well, our Christian Council got involved in local affairs. Traffic accidents, for example, were taking place on average once a month at the main street junction next to my own church. This led to letters being sent to the Town Clerk and Chief Constable not as from some complaining individual, but from united local churches. The trouble was quickly dealt with.

The 'week of prayer for unity' service very soon reached

such proportions that it had to be held in the Roman Catholic church—which served a large district—for the other buildings would not have accommodated the crowds that turned up. The Pope had permitted his people to pray with their 'divided brethren', and the numbers of the former who came to our functions, and the friendliness and joy which they showed, indicated how much many of them had awaited the day when they could pray with the rest of us.

On Sunday night 'service' occasions, rather than weeknight prayer gatherings, we used an abbreviated form of the service sheet devised by the British Council of Churches. The problem of getting permission for preachers of other denominations to use your church was easily by-passed. As we moved round our respective church buildings we simply arranged that the preacher would always belong to the staff of the church in which we were holding our service. And it was very impressive, for at least some people, to hear priests and ministers of 'suspect' denominations all preaching *not* about Church unity, but simple sermons about following Jesus.

The keener you are to share your own joy in Christ with other people the harder do you feel the weight of sheer unbelief and indifference. Hence the joy was all the greater, when going round the parish, to meet in the street a fellow Christian. Often one couldn't remember at first which of the other churches he or she belonged to. Somehow, in the joy of a wee roadside 'crack' together, it didn't seem to matter so much. And as we got to know each other, it was interesting to discover that almost everyone on the local Community Centre council was drawn from that minority—the keen members of the local churches.

Guidance through silence

At Christian Council meetings of course suggestions often arose for further co-operative action. If anyone hesitated, the matter was at once dropped. After all, every one of us was keen to unite as far as possible, but uncertainties naturally arose. Could one agree to that newly-voiced idea, and yet remain loyal to some principle which might not be man's but God's? None of us pretended to be theologians, and we were at times painfully aware of our own ignorance. But after not only private prayer, but our shared silent times together, doubts would often vanish inexplicably. And what had at first caused anxiety now was accepted with joy. Somehow, whenever one felt the local churches had gone as far as we could in all conscience, a way was opened up for a further step forward.

It was the joy of all this that was a great surprise to some of us. And it was obvious that our local churches had become more than three separate 'families'; we were like related married couples, each keeping their own privacy in some things, but all related and 'in and out' of each others' houses. If, for example, you needed help with some youth organiza-tion, you naturally appealed to one of the other churches in the council; and all of us rejoiced over each others' building operations or other signs of development.

After experience of silent prayer with various groups it seems very clear to me, at least, that our forward movement in those early days was the direct result of *passive dependence on the Holy Spirit.* Those silent half-hours together were of prime importance, for they expressed something for which no amount of vocal prayer and hymn-singing could be a sub-stitute. Most people find the latter practice so much easier, and are liable to give in to temptation. But this particular experiment in Christian unity has gone from strength to strength, and today 'is far beyond' the early stage, as one member has written.

After four centuries of sectarian strife since the Reforma-tion, do we really think that Christian unity is going to be achieved by human ingenuity, however much inspired? As Cardinal Bea put it, 'The door to unity is entered on our knees.'[1] And there are times when the sense of the truth of God's majesty is so great, and our littleness so small, that only silence can result. And when that truth is grasped, the light of other truths begins to dawn.

10 *INTO THE FUTURE*
A hymn of faith and courage

They were so certain about things, those Victorians. Quite
unlike our present, doubting, questioning 'age of change'. Or
so it may seem—superficially. The more a person tries to live
by our Maker's Handbook, the Bible, and develop his conscience by obeying it, the more sensitive should he become.
After all, most gospel teaching is as clear as the black print
on the white paper. It is often just our fear that causes us to
doubt that. We may discuss at length this or that puzzling
passage, but the latter are relatively few. The more we try
to live by Jesus' teaching the clearer it becomes. And no
one can do that without great agony of heart and mind
—which is all part of taking up one's cross and following
Christ.

It's easy to run away from controversial issues, and fortify
oneself in a concrete pillbox of dogmatic, unquestioned
opinions. Lazy-mindedness is just as bad, for it breaks the
command to love God with all one's mind. Issues have to be
faced squarely.

And that's what Norman Macleod, the younger, did. He
lived through a time of fierce controversy when his own
Church of Scotland was split from top to bottom at the
Disruption in 1843. The issue at stake need not concern us
here, except to say that it was no trivial matter. Ministers all
over Scotland left the security of their manses and churches,
and whole congregations supported them. (One of my own
grandfather's earliest memories was, as a little kilted laddie,
wandering about among the grown-ups' legs at open-air
services that year.)

Quite obviously this costly adherence to principle was
widely admired, and those ministers who remained within
the established Church suffered criticism. The latter's defence

of their position could be viewed as hypocritical cant, in an attempt to justify their following the easier way. And a man like Norman Macleod would have felt that acutely, for his conscience told him not to desert—as he felt—his Church.

There is a medieval saying that 'God speaks one word and man hears two.' God sees life as a whole; we only see its parts. The 1843 schism has now been almost entirely healed. And who can deny that perhaps some Christians were called to stand for one complementary principle, and others for another? If this factor were more widely recognized there would be far less of that disastrous lack of charity that too often blemishes the Church's life.

Norman Macleod had trained under the famous Thomas Chalmers in Edinburgh, and spent the latter part of his life as minister of the Barony Church, Glasgow. He was especially concerned with the plight of the poor in that growing city, and in all kinds of ways he worked for them. He also edited Christian journals, and one year was moderator of the General Assembly.

His famous and popular hymn will perhaps make a fitting conclusion to our studies as, undaunted, we face the future. No one can reach the calmness of trusting in God except by the hard path of testing; and Macleod's plea to 'do the right' comes from a man who obviously walked humbly with Christ and was therefore ready to concede that he might at times be wrong. But till he was proved wrong, he would stick to his principles, come what may.

> Courage, brother! do not stumble,
>   Though thy path be dark as night;
> There's a star to guide the humble:
>   'Trust in God, and do the right.'
> Let the road be rough and dreary,
>   And its end far out of sight,
> Foot it bravely; strong or weary,
>   Trust in God, and do the right.

Perish policy and cunning,
   Perish all that fears the light!
Whether losing, whether winning,
   Trust in God, and do the right.
Some will hate thee, some will love thee,
   Some will flatter, some will slight;
Cease from man, and look above thee:
   Trust in God, and do the right.

Simple rule, and safest guiding,
   Inward peace, and inward might,
Star upon our path abiding,—
   Trust in God, and do the right.
Courage, brother! do not stumble,
   Though thy path be dark as night;
There's a star to guide the humble:
   'Trust in God, and do the right.'[1]

NOTES

INTRODUCTION

1 Tennyson, *Idylls of the King*, 'The Passing of Arthur', l. 408.
2 Heb. 12.27.
3 Macleod, D., *Memoir of N. Macleod*, vol. i, pp. 289f, quoted in Henderson, G. D., *Mystics of the North-East* (Aberdeen, 1934), p. 37.
4 'To a louse'.
5 Carden, J., *Morning Noon and Night* (Church Missionary Society, 1976), p. 18: the first story from T. K. Thomas, the second from J. Michener, *Tales of the South Pacific*.
6 Merton, T., *Contemplative Prayer* (Darton, Longman & Todd, 1973), p. 82.
7 Ware, K., article 'Silence in Prayer' in *Theology and Prayer* ed. Allchin, A. M. (Fellowship of St Alban and St Sergius, 1975), p. 28.
8 MacInnes, J., *The Evangelical Movement in the Highlands of Scotland 1688–1800* (Aberdeen, 1951), p. 267.
9 Ps. 46.10.
10 Mark 14.37.

1 SPRING FRESHNESS

1 Maclean, A., *Hebridean Altars* (Edinburgh, 1937), p. 125.
2 Waddell, H., *The Wandering Scholars* (Fontana, 1968), p. 62.
3 Bieler, L., *Ireland: Harbinger of the Middle Ages* (Oxford, 1963), p. 65.
4 From the Litany of Dunkeld, 9th century, in Cooper, J., *Reliques of Ancient Scottish Devotion* (Davies, 1934), pp. 24–31.
5 From the Book of Deer, 9th century, ibid., p. 21.
6 Anderson, A. O., & M. O., *Adomnan's Life of Columba* (Nelson, 1961), p. 187.
7 Mackenzie, A. M., *The Foundations of Scotland* (Edinburgh, 1938), p. 35.
8 Lightfoot, J. B., *Leaders in the Northern Church* (London, 1902), p. 9.

9   Eleanor Hull's verse, from Mary Byrne's translation, as in *The Church Hymnary*, Rev. ed., no. 477 (Oxford, 1927).

10 McNeill, J. T., *The Celtic Churches* (Chicago, 1974), p. 25.

11 McLean, G. R. D., *Poems of the Western Highlanders* (S.P.C.K., 1961), no. 434 adapted, from Carmichael, A., *Ortha nan Gaidheal: Carmina Gadelica* (Edinburgh, 1900), i, 32–3.

12 McLean, G. R. D., *Poems of the Western Highlanders Second* (unpublished) from *Carm. Gad.*, iii, 30–31.

13 McLean, *Poems*, no. 1, from *Carm. Gad.*, i, 230–31.

14 Ibid., no. 71, from *Carm. Gad.*, iii, 50–51.

15 Ibid., no. 158, from *Carm. Gad.*, i, 96–7.

16 Ibid., no. 11, from *Carm. Gad.*, iii, 356–7.

17 Ibid., no. 511, from *Carm. Gad.*, i, 84–5.

18 Carmichael, A., *Carm. Gad.*, i, 45.

19 McLean *Poems*, no. 442, from *Carm. Gad.*, i, 330–31.

20 Ibid., no. 308, from *Carm. Gad.*, i, 252–7.

21 Ibid., no. 190, from *Carm. Gad.*, iii, 226–7.

22 Macquarrie, J., *Paths in Spirituality* (S.C.M., 1972), pp. 122–3.

23 Chadwick, N., *The Age of the Saints in the early Celtic Church* (Oxford, 1961), pp. 165,166.

24 Mark 8.36 (AV).

2 GOD IN CREATION

1   From 'The Voice of the Ocean', tr. Patrick McGlynn in *The Owl Remembers*, an anthology selected by John Mackenzie (Stirling, 1933).

2   *Hebridean Altars* (Edinburgh, 1937), p. 123.

3   Ps. 19.1.

4   Matt. 6.26,28.

5   Rom. 1.20.

6   McLean, G. R. D., *Poems of the Western Highlanders* (S.P.C.K., 1961), no. 451. (This book contains new translations of many of the traditional poems in Alexander Carmichael's *Carmina Gadelica*.

7   Ibid., no. 28.

8   From Poem XI in the *Fernaig Manuscript*, ed. Malcolm Macfarlane (Dundee, 1923), tr. the Revd Duncan Mackinnon.

9   *Songs and Hymns of the Scottish Highlands* (Edinburgh, 1888).

Notes

10 From 'The Misty Corrie', tr. Robert Buchanan in *The Book of Highland Verse* ed. D. Mitchell (Paisley, 1912).

11 From the same poem, tr. in Lachlan MacBean's *Songs of the Gael* (Stirling).

12 From 'The Last Adieu to the Hills' tr. R. Buchanan, op. cit.

13 Tr. Professor Blackie in *The Book of Highland Verse*.

14 English composition from the same book.

15 Campbell, J. L., *Father Allan McDonald of Eriskay* (Oliver & Boyd, 1954), p. 13.

16 From 'The Biorlinn of Clanranald' tr. Prof. Blackie in *The Book of Highland Verse*.

17 Campbell, J. L., op. cit., p. 20.

18 From 'The Sugar Brook' by Alexander MacDonald, tr. in Magnus Maclean's *The Literature of the Highlands* (Edinburgh, 1904).

19 McLean, *Poems*, no. 225.

20 Ibid., no. 464.

21 Ibid., no. 449.

22 *Hebridean Altars*, p. 127.

23 *Poems*, no. 306.

24 Matt. 18.3,4,10.

25 From O'Donnell's *Life of Columcille* quoted in Lucy Menzies' *Saint Columba of Iona* (Iona Community, 5th edn, 1970), p. 57.

26 *Poems*, no. 225.

27 The particular occasion described was the late Robert Urqhart Brown's playing at an Aboyne Games, and told me by my own instructor, the late George Gilbert.

28 Thompson, Derick, *An Introduction to Gaelic Poetry* (Gollancz, 1974), p. 263.

29 *Poems*, no. 185.

30 From 'A Love-song to Christ' in Thomson, op. cit., pp. 87–8.

31 *Poems*, no. 351.

3 *VISION OF MANHOOD*

1 Ghéon, H., *The Secret of St Martin* (Sheed and Ward, 1946), p. 8.

2 Menzies, op. cit.; Hale, R. B., *The Magnificent Gael* (World Media Productions, 1976).

3 Anderson, A. O., and M. O., *Adomnan's Life of Columba* (Nelson, 1961).

144

4 This traditional view is challenged by R. B. Hale (see above). Of Columba's passionate nature, however, there can surely be little doubt.

5 Curtis, G., *William of Glasshampton* (S.P.C.K., 1947), p. 150.

6 John 7.17.

7 Eph. 6.10,12.

8 Mark 9.23.

9 Luke 6.26.

4 *SHAKEN INTO TRUTH*

1 Macrae, A., *History of the Clan Macrae* (Dingwall, 1899), pp. 90–91.

2 Ibid., pp. 89–90.

3 Ibid., p. 90.

4 Macrae, D. *A Handful of Lays*, commonly called *The Fernaig Manuscript* ed. Malcolm Macfarlane (Dundee, 1923). Poem no. xiii, tr. the Revd D. Mackinnon.

5 Ibid., no. iv, tr. D. Mackinnon.

6 Ibid., no. ii, tr. D. Mackinnon.

7 Ibid., no. l, tr. the late Dr George Henderson, in *History of the Clan Macrae*, pp. 399–402.

8 Ibid., no. xvii, tr. D. Mackinnon.

9 Ibid., no. viii, tr. D. Mackinnon.

10 Ibid., no. lx, tr. D. Mackinnon.

11 Ibid., no. lxi, tr. D. Mackinnon.

12 Ibid., no. xix, tr. D. Mackinnon.

13 Ibid., no. xxiii, tr. the late Professor Mackinnon, in *History of the Clan Macrae*, pp. 393–5.

14 Ibid., no. lxv, tr. D. Mackinnon.

15 Ibid., no. vi, tr. D. Mackinnon.

16 Ibid., no. xviii, tr. D. Mackinnon.

17 Ibid., no. v, tr. D. Mackinnon.

5 *STILL WATERS RUN DEEP*

1 Henderson, G. D., *Mystics of the North-East* (Aberdeen, 1934). This, and subsequent quotations about Garden's life, from pp. 32–7.

2 Ibid. These two letters are on pp. 208–21, and 237–62.

6 *BEYOND THE MOUNTAINS*

1 Bulloch, J., *Adam of Dryburgh* (SPCK, 1958), p. 54.

2 Kirchberger, C., *Richard of St-Victor: Selected Writings on Contemplation* (Faber, 1957), pp. 30, 31.

3 Ibid. All quotations in this section are taken from Miss Kirchberger's translations of his treatise *Of the four degrees of passionate charity*.

4 Ibid. The following quotations are taken from *Benjamin Minor*.

5 Ibid. The remaining quotations in this study of Richard are from *Benjamin Major*.

7 *WITH GOD IN THE WILDERNESS*

1 Carmichael, A., *Carmina Gadelica* (Oliver and Boyd, 1941), vol. iv, pp. 330–37 (Gaelic and English).

2 John 8.12.

3 Deut. 33.27.

4 John 20.29.

5 Luke 5.4.

8 *A CHURCH AHEAD OF OUR TIME*

1 Eccles. 1.8.

2 For example members of different denominations helping to build each other's churches in the early nineteenth century. These little known occurrences remind one of first-hand accounts of Catholic–Protestant co-operation in Northern Ireland today, which rarely if ever find their way into news bulletins.

3 Craven, J. B., *Journals of the Episcopal Visitations of the Right Rev. Robert Forbes, with a History of the Episcopal Church in the Diocese of Ross, ... and a memoir of Bishop R. Forbes* (London, 2nd edn, 1924), pp. 315–16.

4 Archibald, J., *The Historic Episcopate in the Columban Church and in the Diocese of Moray* (Edinburgh, 1893), p. 192.

5 Craven, J. B., *Records of the Dioceses of Argyll and the Isles 1560–1860* (Kirkwall, 1907), p. 364. I am assured by Mr James MacDonald, Bridge of Coe, that 'Col' in this quotation must be a misprint for 'Coe', and I have consequently emended it.

6 Craven, J. B., *History of the Episcopal Church in the Diocese of Moray* (London, 1889), p. 122.

7   Archibald, J., *History of the Episcopal Church at Keith* (Edinburgh, 1890), p. 70.

8   *Church Times*, 5 March 1976.

9   *Scotland and Scotsmen in the Eighteenth Century from the MSS of John Ramsay Esq. of Ochtertyre* quoted in Eeles, F.C., *Traditional Ceremonial and Customs connected with the Scottish liturgy* (London, 1910), p. 106.

10 *Narrative of Cosmo Innes Esq., Gordon's Shaw* ii, 21, quoted in Craven, *Moray* p. 173.

11 Proceed down road to Brin from Dunlichity church; cross burn, and then a smaller stream (more like a ditch). Just beyond this watercourse, on your right, is the stone once used as a font. Proceed a little along the road and the ground rises to your left; at the top of this rise is the hollow. Before visiting the hollow please obtain permission from Mr J. Shaw, Tordarroch House.

12 Half way between Ballachulish bridge and St John's Church, Ballachulish, the road crosses a broad ditch (now narrowed by road works) which runs into the wooded grounds of Craigrannoch house by the shore of Loch Leven. This ditch is Laggan na Bann (Hollow of the Bond), not 'Laggan-a-bhainne': so am I informed by Mr Malcolm Robertson, Ballachulish. Here disputes were settled amicably between local clans, and services held in secret. Another site is Rudha na Glaistig (the Goblin's Point) which is the largest promontory reaching out into Loch Leven behind the old railway station; the people met for worship here among the hillocks.

13 Archibald, *Keith*, op. cit., p. 82.

14 Craven, *Argyll*, op. cit., pp. 327–8.

15 Craven, *Journals*, op. cit., p. 112.

16 Ibid., p. 352.

17 Donaldson, M.E.M., *Scotland's Suppressed History* (London, 1935), pp. 341–5.

18 Ibid., pp. 332–5.

19 Craven, *Journals*, op. cit., pp. 290–91.

20 *Scottish Guardian*, 1865, quoted in Craven, *Journals*, p. 129.

21 Eeles, *Traditional Ceremonial*, p. 94.

22 Craven, *Journals*, op. cit., p. 182.

23 Medwyn, Lord, *Biographical Sketch of Alexander, Lord Pitsligo* quoted in Pratt, J., *Buchan* (Aberdeen, 1858), p. 388.

24 This is traditional in Glencoe. See also article by Dr W. Ferguson in *The Scottish Historical Review*, vol. xlvi, 1 : No.141: April, 1967.

25 MacDonald, A., *The Clan Donald*, vol. ii (Inverness, 1901).

26 Craven, *Journals*, op. cit., p. 305.

27 Donaldson, *Suppressed History*, p. 282.

28 Forbes, R., *The Lyon in Mourning*, edited by H. Paton, vol. iii (Edinburgh, 1895), p. 132. (One of the best portraits of Prince Charlie is by Pettie, and shows him with two companions—Lochiel and Pitsligo).

29 Ingram, M., *A Jocobite Stronghold of the Church* (Edinburgh, 1907).

30 Forbes, op. cit., p. 115.

31 First quotation from *The Scots Magazine*, Nov., 1773, quoted in the same journal Jan., 1974. The second quotation from *Johnson's Journey to the Western Islands of Scotland*, edited by Chapman, R. W. (Oxford, 1930), p. 95.

32 Quoted in Mackenzie, A. M., *The Passing of the Stewarts* (Edinburgh, 1937), p. 403.

33 Voillaume, R., *Brothers of Men* (Darton, Longman & Todd, 1966), ch. 5.

34 Daiches, D., *The Paradox of Scottish Culture* (Oxford, 1964), pp. 52–5.

35 Campbell, J. F., *Popular Tales of the West Highlands* (Paisley, 1890), vol. iv, p. 72.

36 Carmichael, A., op. cit., p. 347.

37 Walker, J., *The life and Times of John Skinner* (London, 1883), p. 149.

38 Fairweather, B., *A Short History of Ballachulish Slate Quarry* (The Glencoe and North Lorn Folk Museum), p. 4.

39 Archibald, *Keith*, op. cit., p. 74.

40 Craven, *Moray*, op. cit., p. 305.

41 Craven, *Journals*, op. cit., p. 95.

42 Craven, *Argyll*, op. cit., p. 196.

43 Forbes, op. cit., pp. 3–11 and 22.

44 Craven, *Journals*, op. cit., p. 46.

45 I am informed by Mr Robertson that the building was Laroch stables and not the 'storehouse' at St John's Church.

46 *Scottish Ecclesiastical Journal*, 22 July 1858: quoted in Craven, *Moray*, op. cit., pp. 279–80.

47 MacGillivray, A. *A Short History of St Paul's Episcopal Church, Strathnairn*, with later additional material up till 1955 (Inverness).

48 Craven, *Journals*, op. cit., pp. 131–4 for this and subsequent quotations.

49 Ibid., p. 113.

50 Craven, *Moray*, op. cit., p. 280.

51 Notes in St Paul's Church vestry, Strathnairn.

52 Craven, *Journals*, op. cit., pp. 101, 103.

53 Craven, *Moray*, op. cit., p. 105.

54 Ibid., p. 126.

55 Craven, *Journals*, op. cit., pp. 128–9.

56 Walker, J., *The Life of the Rt Revd Alexander Jolly* (Edinburgh, 1878), p. 38.

57 Ibid., pp. 99–100.

58 Craven, *Journals*, op. cit., pp. 245–6.

59 Walker, *Skinner*, op. cit., p. 92.

60 Ramsay, Dean, *Reminiscences of Scottish Life and Character*, 22nd edn (Edinburgh, 1872), p. 45.

61 *Spalding Club Miscellany*, ii, 297, quoted in Craven, *Moray*, p. 71.

62 Archibald, *Moray*, op. cit., p. 222.

63 Henderson, G. D., op. cit., p. 35.

64 2 Cor. 12.10.

65 Craven, *Argyll*, op. cit., p. 155.

Apart from general history books, most of the information in this study has been drawn from the above-mentioned sources. Those who wish to consult a brief and concise historical account of Scotland's church history in the eighteenth century could read Agnes Mure Mackenzie's *The Passing of the Stewarts* (Edinburgh, 1937), sec. iii. Although it only covers the first half of that century, it clarifies the issues at stake.

9 *UNITY THROUGH SILENT PRAYER*

1 Quoted in Suenens, J. L., *A New Pentecost?* (Darton, Longman & Todd, 1975), p. 185.

10 *INTO THE FUTURE*

1 *The Church Hymnary*, rev. edn (Oxford, 1927), no. 529.

P. 23.